TRUTHS
LIE

Forces
of Nature

AMMI-JOAN PAQUETTE
and LAURIE ANN THOMPSON

WALDEN POND PRESS
An Imprint of HarperCollinsPublishers

Walden Pond Press is an imprint of HarperCollins Publishers.
Walden Pond Press and the skipping stone logo are trademarks and registered trademarks of Walden Media, LLC.

Two Truths and a Lie: Forces of Nature
Text copyright © 2019 by Ammi-Joan Paquette and Laurie Ann Thompson
Illustrations copyright © 2019 by Lisa K. Weber
All rights reserved. Manufactured in Europe.
No part of this book may be used or reproduced in any manner whatsoever without written permission except in the case of brief quotations embodied in critical articles and reviews. For information address HarperCollins Children's Books, a division of HarperCollins Publishers, 195 Broadway, New York, NY 10007.
www.harpercollinschildrens.com
ISBN 978-0-06-241883-8 (trade bdg.) — ISBN 978-0-06-241884-5 (pbk.)
Typography by Cara Llewellyn
20 21 22 23 24 GPS 10 9 8 7 6 5 4 3 2 1
❖
First Edition

For my amazing, tireless, eagle-eyed coauthor, Laurie:
I could not have done it without you!
—Joan

To Joan, for sharing your ideas, talents, hard work, and friendship.
There's no one I'd rather be taking this journey with.
—Laurie

CONTENTS

INTRODUCTION

There's something reassuring about opening a nonfiction book and knowing that all the stories and people you will read about are real; that everything between those covers is entirely factual. There's also something exciting about opening a novel and knowing that all the stories and people you will read about inside are imaginary; in that world, there is no limit to the adventures that can take place.

But what if—just go with us for a second here—*what if* you could blend up a delicious bookshake to combine the very best of both of these elements?

Welcome to *Two Truths and a Lie*—the book series that tells you *to* think, not *what* to think!

Here's the scoop: Every scintillating, science-packed chapter in this book contains three stories. Two of these stories are 100% true and you can believe them fully. But one of the stories . . . is not. Beware of that story! It might contain true bits, might name actual people or events or explain true concepts. But in every chapter, there will be one story that overall—its main point, direction, or idea—is fake, false, kaput.

The tasks set before you are simple: Read. Reflect. Research.

And then pass judgment on what you have read. Is the story true or false? Fact or fake? Cross your heart or cross your fingers?

Once you think you've got it figured out, you can flip on over to the back of the book to check your answers. But be careful not to peek ahead . . . you wouldn't want to spoil the fun, would you?

We're not gonna lie (about this, anyway)—digging up the truth will be a challenge! But isn't that true of most of the really good things in life?

Here we go. . . .

PART 1

IT'S ELEMENTAL

When you're talking about science, it's often easiest to start with what's right in front of you: the ground beneath your feet, the water you drink, the air you breathe. The basics. Sounds pretty easy, right? Safe? Comfortable?

Not necessarily.

Mother Nature has quite a few tricks up her sleeve, and you might be surprised at just how extraordinary our planet can be. Want some examples? Read on! Just remember not to believe everything you read. . . .

A. THE PIT OF DESPAIR

Step right up! See the gigantic pit in the Karakum Desert of central Turkmenistan. Be careful, though. Don't get *too* close!

If you were able to peer (very carefully) over the edge, you would see a gaping hole in the ground. It's roughly 225 feet wide (that's as long as six school buses end to end!) and more than 65 feet deep. Flames shoot out from the floor and walls of the crater, but there is no smoke.

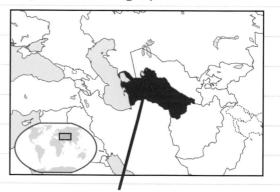

The Darvaza Crater in Turkmenistan

An impressive sight, for sure, if a bit unnerving. Local residents refer to it as the "Door to Hell." (Okay, maybe it's a *lot* unnerving.)

But how did this pit of despair come to be? Many of the exact details are a bit uncertain. Maybe that is simply due to poor record keeping, or perhaps someone didn't want the world to find out the truth. In any case, the story goes something like this. . . .

In 1971, Turkmenistan was still part of the Soviet Union. That year a team of Soviet geologists went out into the desert near the town of Darvaza looking for oil. They selected what looked like a good spot and started drilling. Unfortunately, they did not find oil. Instead, they must have drilled down into an underground cavern filled with natural gas. The ground above the cavern collapsed, swallowing up all the expensive drilling equipment. Luckily, no one was hurt, but their hunt for oil was a bust. All that remained was a huge hole in the ground.

Later, they realized they had an even bigger problem on their hands. Dead animals were being found in the areas surrounding the crater, having **suffocated** from gases seeping out from the new sinkhole. How could they protect the local environment, wildlife, and people? Bingo! They decided to set the whole thing on fire. Within a few weeks, the pocket of gas would burn itself out and everything could return to normal. A perfect solution, right?

Not so much.

Fast-forward *forty years*. Yup—four decades. And that pesky crater? You guessed it . . . It's still burning!

We now know that Turkmenistan has one of the world's largest known natural gas reserves, and those reserves tend to be concentrated in giant underground fields. Gas equals

suffocate: Die from lack of oxygen

fuel, and as long as a fuel source remains, the fire will just keep on burning. No one knows how long this so-called door to the underworld might be shooting out its deadly flames, but one thing's clear: there are no signs of it stopping anytime soon. Oops!

To make the place even more unsettling, spiders have been seen plunging to their dooms by the thousands (maybe in a misguided attempt to get warm?). And there's no fence or warning signs to keep other animal observers—including humans—safe, either.

The pit at twilight

So, you know what? On second thought, maybe *don't* step right up after all. Let's all step *back* instead. This fiery phenomenon might be impressive to witness, but you're probably better off observing it from a safe distance.

Be careful, big fella!

Talk It Out:
Choose Your Own Disaster

Actions—whether our own or others'—have results, and not all of them are good. When things go wrong, there usually isn't much time to think. In the moment, it can be difficult to know what actions to take, even for the experts. That's where thinking ahead comes in. Try this:

1. Imagine a disaster that could happen near where you live (think fire, flood, earthquake, or the like).

2. Research and think critically about actions, responses, and plans. What would you do? What are the safest and most practical strategies toward a solution? What are the advantages of your plan? The disadvantages?

3. Now take it a step further: Are there steps that can be taken to help prevent that disaster from happening?

4. Brainstorm and discuss ideas and solutions together. When you've planned ahead, you can be ready for almost anything!

B. THEY'RE MAIKEN A SPLASH!

Here's a recipe for a perfect day: gather a group of friends; get on a boat; toss up some blue skies, sunshine, and a strong, refreshing breeze. Yep, perfection! Can't you just see it? Nothing but blue as far as the eye can see. Not a single thing.

Except . . .

What is that shadow below the waves?

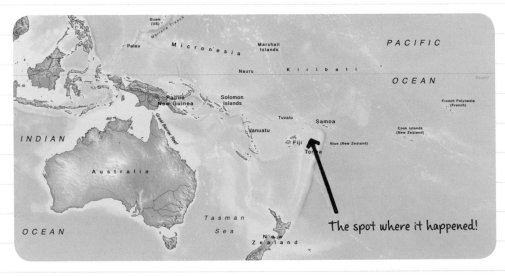

The spot where it happened!

Let's hit pause for a second here. If that all sounded like a **hypothetical** scene, well, it wasn't. In the spring of 2006, Fredrik Fransson and Håkan Larsson set sail from the coast of California in a yacht called the *Maiken*. The sea voyage would span more than six months and would take the friends 6,000 nautical miles: from the west coast of North America clear across the Pacific Ocean to Australia. An adventurous journey to be sure, and the crew would document their travels on their blog along the way whenever they were able to get online.

The trip was full of excitement and wonder. But one experience would quickly surpass all the others. It was early afternoon on August 11, when the *Maiken* was sailing near Fiji in the South Pacific. Something caught the crew's attention: instead of its usual open-sea blue, the water around them looked murky and green.

As the plot thickened, so did the water. No, really! The sea took on a brown and grainy texture. As Fransson wrote in his blog entry, "the sea turned to stone"!

Sailing through a sea of stones

Not literally, of course—but very quickly, the boat was engulfed by a thick raft of **pumice** stones floating along the surface of the water.

What was going on? Unbeknownst to the crew, the real excitement was happening far below: just a couple miles away, deep under the sea, a volcano was erupting.

An eruption above ground might spew rock and lava into the air and onto the surrounding countryside; underwater, however, it's a different story. There, the rocky matter piles up and up to form a seamount. If there's enough of it, the new landmass crests up out of the water.

Presto! We have an island.

It's a brand-new baby island!

The *Maiken*'s crew quickly realized they were witness to something extraordinary—the formation of a new island, happening right before their eyes, in real time. Not far from where they sailed, an explosion shot a plume of black smoke into the air. Then another. And each rumble sent a wedge of land rising up and up. The sea was very busy that day, maiken' an island. And the friends were among the very few humans to witness such an amazing birth.

When the photos were posted online, people

hypothetical: Something that's possible or that could happen

pumice: Lightweight volcanic rock formed by fast-cooling frothy lava

Incredible Islands

Expansive ocean views, blowing winds, beaches . . . Whether it's just off the coast or way out in the middle of the ocean, being on an island is an unusual experience for most of us. There's even a word for people who are obsessed with them: islomania! Here are some islands we think are pretty impressive (and one we just made up):

1. Fadiouth, Senegal: almost entirely covered by clamshells

2. Miyakejima, Japan: poisonous gases coming up from the ground force residents to carry gas masks

3. San Serriffe, Indian Ocean: boats continually carry sand from the east coast to the west to manage the constant erosion

4. Thilafushi, Maldives: an ever-expanding dump receiving about 31,000 truckloads of trash a year

5. Tashirojima, Japan: more feline inhabitants than people (and no dogs allowed!)

6. Bishop Rock, United Kingdom: perhaps the world's smallest island to have a building on it

(Continued on next page)

around the world took notice. Scientists from NASA scrambled to verify the discovery and reach the island—while they still could. Why the rush? While it's not uncommon for a new island to form, it is unusual for it to last. Most new islands slip back below the waves within a few months of their birth.

Sadly, that was to be the case with this fledgling island. While the eruption and birth were verified by satellite and tracking mechanisms—an image of the island and the pumice raft was published on NASA's Earth Observatory—by a year later, all hard evidence was gone.

Gone, but not forgotten. Thanks to the crew of the

Maiken, this amazing act of creation was seen not just by them, but by all of us through their eyes, too.

A perfect end to an extraordinarily perfect day.

Yep, there's ocean under that pumice!

A WHIRL WITHOUT A POOL

Imagine yourself hiking through the Sahara Desert in Africa. A hot, dry wind is blowing. As far as you can see in any direction, there's nothing but sand dunes, stretching away for miles. What you wouldn't give for a cool drink of water! Well, you certainly won't find any water here.

At least, not anymore.

Wait—what?

It's true! Millions of years ago the Sahara Desert looked and felt *very* different than it does today. You might already know that the Earth is constantly remaking itself. Rearranged by **plate tectonics**, the continents'

The location of the Richat Structure

locations have shifted and their shapes have changed. Other forces have contributed, too, such as volcanoes that pushed **magma** up from the Earth's interior and glaciers that crept across its surface. And it's not just the Earth's landmasses that have moved around. Oceans and seas have undergone their own transformations.

Still, it might surprise you to learn that one of the driest places on Earth was once located at the bottom of an ocean. That's right: the area now known as the Sahara Desert used to be completely covered over by water. Geologists have known this for a long time, of course. I mean, where else could all that sand have come from? Many marine fossils have been found there, too, even whale skeletons! But one question remained . . . where did all the water go?

The shocking yet simple answer was finally revealed thanks to photos taken from space. Astronauts were the first people to see the strange and beautiful geological feature now known as the Richat Structure, or Eye of Africa. Located outside of Ouadane, Mauritania, in northwestern Africa, it's about 30 miles wide. That means it would take you about ten hours to walk all the way across it (as long as you don't stop for a long water break).

But be careful, you don't want

plate tectonics: A theory that the Earth's surface is made up of large, floating pieces that interact with each other

magma: Molten rock

to get sucked in! Geologists believe that the Richat Structure is what's left of a giant, ancient drain. It seems that at some point there was, literally, a hole in the bottom of the sea. And the ocean that used to cover the Sahara Desert was sucked down this hole right back into the Earth's crust. Eventually, the water must have cooled the magma enough to create a natural stone plug in the great drain, leaving behind the Sahara Desert and the impressive Eye of Africa, massive enough to be seen from space.

Too bad we don't have pictures of it from when it was draining.

Try It: Make Your Own Whirlpools

Are you ready to get wet in the name of science? To start, you'll need to collect some clear plastic bottles, duct tape, dish soap, and vegetable oil.

First, fill one bottle about two-thirds full of water. Place an empty bottle opening-to-opening with the first bottle and duct tape them together (try to make sure they won't leak). Over a sink or bathtub (in case of leaks!), quickly turn the bottles over. Did you make a whirlpool? No, probably not. In fact, the water probably didn't move much at all! Now, do the same thing again, but this time give the bottles a good swirl. Notice how much better the water can move after you create a whirlpool!

Repeat the process, but this time add some dish soap to the water before taping the bottles together. Experiment with dish soap whirlpools.

Repeat the process again, but this time add the oil instead of the soap. Can you explain what you're seeing?

Imagine what all that swirling water would have looked like . . . It must have been the world's most enormous whirlpool ever! A pity for any poor creatures that might have gotten caught up in its powerful currents, though.

These days the pool is long gone and all that's left is the whorl. One thing is certain: You won't drown while crossing the Sahara Desert . . . but please do make sure to bring along enough water to drink.

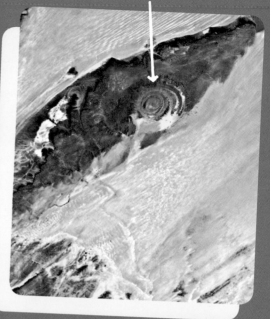

Image taken by Envisat's Medium Resolution Imaging Spectrometer (MERIS)

YOU'VE JUST READ THREE *weird and wacky stories about our Earth: a giant hole in the ground that has been burning for more than forty years, a brand-new island that formed right before the eyes of a ship's lucky crew, and an ancient whirlpool that drained away the sea and left behind the Sahara Desert. Two of those stories are actually true, but one of them most definitely is not. Can you guess which of the three is the fake?*

ICE-CAPADES

So there you are, on a ship chugging through the ice-cold waters of the Arctic Ocean. Up ahead you notice the surface of the water is covered with glistening white . . . flowers? What are they? Where did they come from?

That's exactly what fishermen in the polar regions have been wondering for centuries, but thanks to new research, we're finally getting some answers.

Up close with some frost flowers

The delicate blossoms are called frost flowers, but they're definitely not plants. They're actually a rare and beautiful kind of sea ice, one that can form only under specific, unusual weather conditions. First, it has to be oh-so-very cold. Like, *way*-below-freezing cold. Brrrr! Then, the ocean has to turn to ice, but just in a thin layer at the very surface. Finally, there has to be a hailstorm.

That's right: hail. When the hail hits the super-thin sheet of ice on top of the ocean, it breaks right on through the delicate crust. That causes a splash of water to shoot out of the resulting hole. But since the air above the ice layer is so cold, the splashing water

freezes in place, leaving behind a beautiful icy "flower." Each small ball of hail makes its own frost flower. Those frost flowers lower the surface temperature of the ocean even more, so the splashes from bigger and bigger balls of hail are able to be frozen solid—resulting in bigger and bigger frost flowers. This process stops only when the hailstorm ends, sometimes leaving the ocean covered in frost flowers as far as the eye can see!

But that's not all: researchers from the University of Washington's Ocean Sciences department have spent the last

Freshly formed frost flowers

Try It: Fast Frozen Fun

Here's a simple but totally cool science experiment you can do to amaze your family and friends. You'll need an ice cube, a piece of string or yarn, a cup or bowl of water, and some table salt. Place the ice cube in the cup of water. Lay part of the string on the ice cube. Sprinkle salt over the string where it touches the ice cube. Wait about ten seconds, then lift up the string. The ice cube should now be attached!

How does it work? The salt lowers the freezing temperature of the ice, which makes it start to melt. The string sinks down into the melted puddle. As more of the ice melts, it makes the water less salty. Less salty water can freeze more easily, so some of the water freezes again—with the string inside it!

For even more science fun, try using different sizes of salt (like sea salt, rock salt, or kosher salt) or different kinds of salt (like Epsom salt or baking soda) to see if they behave differently.

six years studying the frost flower phenomenon, and they've discovered some even more interesting facts about them. For instance, because there is a layer of **brine** at the surface of the ocean, frost flowers are about three times saltier than the bodies of water in which they are found. And what do you get when you let a frost flower melt? Water, of course! But scientists were surprised to find that you'll *also* get about a million bacteria in each

brine: Very salty water

and every frost flower—a much higher concentration than you'll find in normal seawater. Researchers haven't quite figured out how the bacteria get there or why they're so numerous; perhaps they hitch a ride on the hailstones?

That's just one of the many mysteries that the researchers are trying to solve. They're also looking at what happens when the frost flowers eventually melt in the ocean: How is the surrounding water changed, and is there any effect on the atmosphere? What happens to the bacteria—do they survive in their new environment, and do they cause any problems there? Unfortunately, all of these questions are extremely difficult to answer, since the conditions that cause frost flowers are so uncommon, unpredictable, and—did we mention?—oh-so-very cold.

These frost flowers were made by researchers

So, the next time you happen to be out cruising the Arctic Ocean in a hailstorm and stumble upon a field of frost flowers, maybe try carefully scooping up a few in the name of science. Just don't forget to put them in the freezer!

B. THE PARTING OF THE JINDO SEA

There is a legend in South Korea that says that Jindo Island—a small island off the southern tip of Korea—was once inhabited by tigers. When the tigers started threatening a village, the people there escaped by raft to the nearby Modo Island. Unfortunately, in their hurry to leave, an elderly grandmother was accidentally left behind. Every day she prayed to the god of the ocean to be safely reunited with her loved ones. Eventually, the god appeared to her in a dream and said he would send a rainbow to the sea so she could cross the ocean. The next day, the sea parted and the woman joined

Jindo Island

her family and friends once again . . . by walking right across the seafloor!

Whether the legend is true or not, the waters of the Jindo Sea really do part—enough for people to walk from Jindo to Modo Island and back again.

Scientists say there are several reasons for this phenomenon (none of which involve hungry tigers, thank goodness). The first has to do with tides: the continuous rising and falling of the

Looking out across the parting sea

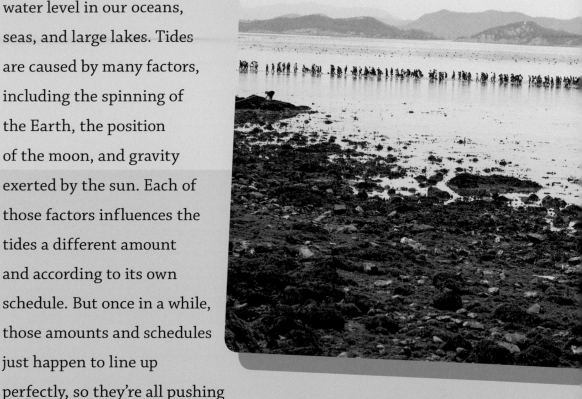

water level in our oceans, seas, and large lakes. Tides are caused by many factors, including the spinning of the Earth, the position of the moon, and gravity exerted by the sun. Each of those factors influences the tides a different amount and according to its own schedule. But once in a while, those amounts and schedules just happen to line up perfectly, so they're all pushing or pulling the water in the same direction at the same time. When the sea parts at Jindo, it is because the water is being pulled away from the islands and farther out to sea.

The second reason people can walk from Jindo Island to Modo Island during this special time is that there is an underwater ridge of land connecting the two islands. Because the ocean is calmer between the two islands, sand gets deposited there. Over time, the sand has built up high enough to become exposed—kind of like a bridge—when the tides cause the water to get extremely low.

Gradually, as the water recedes, what was hidden beneath the waves is transformed into a temporary road through the sea.

The path, nearly two miles long and usually over 100 feet wide (about the length of two train cars parked end to end), is big enough that hundreds of thousands of tourists from around the world can get a glimpse of it when they visit every spring. Some even get a chance to walk back and forth between the two islands. Timing is everything here, though, as the "road" may only be open for an hour or so before the water returns and the islands become actual islands once more. Better hurry, folks!

Part of the Jindo Miracle Sea Road Festival

Fortunately, all those people have something to do before and after the brief parting of the sea. Every year, Jindo County hosts the Jindo Miracle Sea Road Festival, a four-day celebration for locals and visitors alike. The festival features traditional art performances, parades, exhibitions, and other events to entertain and delight guests.

And, indeed, it all does sound pretty delightful, doesn't it? I mean, as long as nobody forgets Grandma . . . and there aren't any ravenous tigers lurking around!

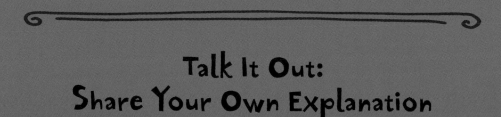

Talk It Out:
Share Your Own Explanation

Throughout history, human beings have invented stories to explain things they didn't understand. Take a minute to think about something interesting in nature (like frost flowers! or parting seas!). Whether you know the real reasons behind it or not doesn't matter: you can be as scientific or imaginative as you like! What other explanations might you be able to imagine for that phenomenon? What ideas might you come up with if you were encountering that occurrence for the first time? Share your thoughts with others, and listen to theirs!

Remember, however, to be honest with your listeners. If you're making things up, be sure everyone knows it! Fiction can certainly be fun, but you don't want to spread misinformation or false facts.

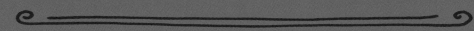

C. A (MOSTLY) LETHAL LAKE

Are you looking for a nifty new vacation spot? You might consider Lake Natron. First, it's located in the scenic Great Rift Valley in Tanzania. Second, the water is usually the perfect temperature for swimming, around 80 degrees Fahrenheit. And, we saved the best part for last: it's a *soda lake*. Doesn't that sound delicious? Somebody bring me a straw!

Unfortunately, it's not *that* kind of soda. In this case, soda means a chemical compound containing sodium—not a sugary carbonated beverage! This lake, in fact, just might kill you . . . and anything else that happens to get too close to it. So, maybe *not* the ideal vacation spot after all!

Lake Natron

Why is Lake Natron so deadly? The soda we're talking about here is actually sodium carbonate, a chemical used in soaps, cleaners, and many other things. Have you ever accidentally gotten soap in your eyes? Well, the water in Lake Natron is so **caustic** that it can burn the skin and eyes of most animals—including people. This is all thanks to a nearby volcano, Ol Doinyo Lengai, which is the only volcano in the world to spew a type of runny black lava and ash that is rich in sodium carbonate. Rain washes the lava and ash into the lake, making it more **alkaline**.

One neat, if creepy, side effect of the high level of sodium carbonate in the water is that it preserves and encrusts everything that happens to die in it. So the lake kills things . . . and then it turns their bodies into "stone." These corpse statues are revealed when the lake's water level drops in the dry season. In 2012, wildlife photographer Nick Brandt happened to be there to see it, and he captured the freaky phenomenon on film. He collected the

Yes, the lake turns red!

crystallized bodies exactly as he found them, then placed them in various scenes as though they were still alive before taking his striking photographs: perched on a branch, sunbathing on a rock, or floating gracefully on the surface of the water.

As weird—and deadly—as Lake Natron is, some things do live there. Salt-loving bacteria and algae flourish, periodically turning the lake waters a deep red. A unique

caustic: Able to chemically burn or destroy living tissue

alkaline: The opposite of acidic; like bleach

Flamingos enjoying a day at the lake

species of fish has adapted to the harsh conditions and thrives in the lake, with absolutely no worries about competition or predators. Lake Natron is also the primary breeding ground for the lesser flamingo. When the water level is just right, more than two million of these birds will make nests on temporary salt islands that form in the middle of the lake during the dry season. The lake then acts as a moat, protecting the nests from predators. The adult flamingos feast on the lake's red algae, which gives them their vivid pink color.

If we're going to protect those species, then their

Spectacular Lakes

Lakes are not just oversize puddles of water. They can be as small as a pond or as large as a sea, crystal clear or dark and muddy, life-giving or deadly. They come in varying shapes, sizes, and chemical makeups. Our Earth has millions of lakes, but here are a few of the more unusual ones. All of these are real . . . except one! Can you guess which?

1. Plitvice Lakes, Croatia: 16 lakes connected by waterfalls, called one of the most beautiful places in the world

2. Lake Hillier, Western Australia: bright pink in color due to algae that release a red pigment

3. Spotted Lake, British Columbia, Canada: covered in large multicolored discs due to minerals

4. Spiral Lake, Guatemala: viewed from the air, it's a perfect spiral shape

5. Five Flower Lake, China: clear and shallow, displaying a rainbow of colors

6. Abraham Lake, Alberta, Canada: in the winter, filled with frozen bubbles of methane gas

7. Jellyfish Lake, Palau, Micronesia: yep, you guessed it . . . filled with jellyfish

8. Lake Baikal, Siberia, Russia: the deepest, and possibly oldest, lake in the world

9. Dead Sea, Middle East: actually a lake, yet about ten times saltier than the ocean

10. Lake Nyos, Cameroon: sits atop a pocket of magma, capable of exploding and releasing deadly amounts of carbon dioxide

unique habitat needs protection, too. Conservation groups are keeping a close eye on the area around Lake Natron after hearing about one proposal to build a hydroelectric dam and a separate plan to extract the soda ash for industrial use. Either of those activities could alter the lake's water levels and chemistry, which could possibly endanger both the flamingos and the one-of-a-kind fish population.

Conservationists would prefer you don't actually vacation there either, since too many tourists would cause other environmental problems for the entire area. So, despite the interesting statuary you might find lying on the beach at Lake Natron . . . we highly recommend you drink your soda elsewhere.

FROZEN FROST FLOWERS MADE *by hail, a predictable parting of the ocean that reveals a temporary land bridge between two islands, or a lake that both kills and preserves almost everything it touches . . . Which one of these stories is just too unbelievable? Which two do you think might be true? Do your own research to know for sure!*

A. KRAKATAU'S LOUD LAST WORDS

It began on August 26, 1883, a Sunday evening, when the first in a series of major explosions rocked the area around the Krakatau volcano (also known as Krakatoa) in Indonesia. Then, at exactly 10:02 a.m. local time on August 27, came the fourth and final boom. And what a boom it was.

Krakatau erupting

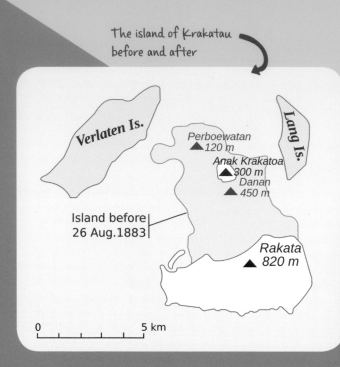

The island of Krakatau
before and after

Verlaten Is.

Lang Is.

Perboewatan
▲ 120 m

Anak Krakatoa
▲ 300 m

Danan
▲ 450 m

Island before
26 Aug. 1883

Rakata
▲ 820 m

0   5 km

The eruption blew the volcano—along with most of its island—completely off the map. (That's right . . . it was, quite literally, gone!) The event was, and still is, one of the most powerful volcanic eruptions in human history.

Scientists estimate that the total explosive force of the eruptions was about the same as two hundred megatons of **TNT**. That's as much as ten thousand times more powerful than the explosion from an atomic bomb! At least five cubic miles of dust and debris were shot into the atmosphere, which blocked out the sun in the area for almost three days. This ash eventually circled the planet, causing vividly colorful skies in Europe and North America and a drop in average global temperatures that lasted for years.

Some of the most surprising effects, however, weren't those that could be seen or felt—they were ones that could be heard. The

TNT: Trinitrotoluene, a type of explosive

decibel: A unit of measurement of sound volume

final explosion was the loudest sound ever known to have been experienced by humans. It was so loud, in fact, that the sound waves were actually pushing the air along in front of them, instead of traveling through it like normal sounds do. The captain of a ship that was 40 miles away from the eruption wrote, "So violent are the explosions that the eardrums of over half my crew have been shattered."

One hundred miles away, the sound was still measured at 172

decibels. To put that into perspective: anything louder than 130 decibels will have you covering your ears in pain. And the sound kept going: On Rodrigues Island, 3,000 miles away from Krakatau (about the same distance as Los Angeles to Boston), the chief of police thought the sound was "the distant roar of heavy guns." In all, the sound of that volcanic eruption could be heard by people across 13% of the Earth's surface.

Finally the sound itself became too quiet to hear, but the wave of air it was pushing kept right on going. Barographs—instruments that measure and record air pressure over time—showed the proof. Around the world, barograph pens suddenly jerked up, then down, and continued to bounce around for almost two hours. Then they went quiet again. But, like ripples in a small pond, the waves met each other on the other side

This famous painting is said to have been inspired by the effects of the eruption

of the globe and circled back again. This went on for more than five days, and the waves ended up silently traveling around the world no fewer than seven times, moving at a speed of about 675 miles per hour.

So, if a volcano erupts on a distant island but you don't hear it at home, does it really make a sound? The volcano eruption of Krakatau in 1883 most definitely did, and its effects reached people all around the world . . . whether they heard them or not.

Impressive Volcanoes

Volcanoes can be found on every continent, with about 1,500 of them considered to be potentially active. Here are a few of the particularly notable ones (plus one that's not quite real):

1. Vesuvius, Italy: one of the most dangerous on Earth due to its proximity to the nearby city of Naples . . . ever heard of Pompeii?

2. Thrihnukagigur, Iceland: visitors can take an elevator down 400 feet inside an old magma chamber

3. Mauna Loa, Hawaii: the world's largest active volcano

4. Sakurajima, Japan: near-constant eruptions frequently blanket the entire region in ash

5. Kavachi, Solomon Islands: one of the most active underwater volcanoes, also known as "Sharkcano" (because sharks actually live inside it!)

6. Thera, Greece: believed to be the largest eruption ever witnessed by humans, taking place over 3,500 years ago

7. Yellowstone, Wyoming: a supervolcano that could one day trigger the next ice age

8. Nyiragongo, Democratic Republic of Congo: known for its fast-flowing lava, which has moved at more than 60 miles per hour

9. Eyjafjallajökull, Iceland: its 2010 eruption released a giant ash cloud that caused four commercial airplanes to crash into the Atlantic Ocean

10. Vulcan Point, Philippines: world's largest volcano in a lake on a volcano

B. WINDMILLS TO THE RESCUE

Holland: land of colorful tulips, wooden shoes, delicious cheese, and, of course, windmills. As the locals of this region of the western coast of the Netherlands know, however, it also has an abundance

of clouds, rain, and nearly constant moisture. Rain falls in Holland about half the days of the year, and even when it isn't raining, it's often so damp it feels like you're walking around inside a cloud. In addition, residents rarely get to see the bright blue sky because they're tucked away under a solid layer of gloomy gray clouds.

But, finally, there is hope for brighter days ahead.

The Netherlands

The Google office in Amsterdam has announced a rather ingenious plan. You know those aforementioned windmills? Well, Google developers have found a way to put them to even better use. Combined

So many tulips!

with Google's massive online computing capabilities and its expertise in artificial intelligence, the windmills now do more than just harness the weather . . . they can actually *change* it.

Say what?

That's right. Cameras throughout Holland study the clouds and relay the information back to Google's servers. When cloud patterns indicate that rain is in the forecast, the internet-connected windmills respond automatically. By coordinating their spinning, they're able to create massive gusts of wind and shoo the clouds away.

So far, the plan has been working great for Google's Amsterdam office. Employees are happier thanks to the improved weather, which makes them more productive. More sunlight also means more solar energy. In fact, since launching the program, Google's data centers have noted 23% more sunlight hours per solar panel and a 42% reduction in their overall energy costs—good for both profits *and* the environment.

And the benefits reach far beyond Google. To take advantage of the new clean-energy boom, solar capabilities are expanding all over Holland. Less rain also means more tulips—and more tourists—both of which are good for the Dutch economy. And, using weather radar information from all over Europe, the windmills can accurately determine where rain is needed most and blow the clouds in the optimal direction. This means that Holland's windmill system can help other countries by eliminating drought there at the same time they are helping Holland stay clear and dry at home.

Could a system like this benefit other areas of the world? Google thinks so. They're already investigating setting up a similar windmill network in the Olympic Peninsula's temperate rainforest in the Pacific Northwest of the United States. That should make the rain-soaked residents of Seattle and the surrounding regions

Google Cloud logo

Google Cloud

jump for joy, as well as those in the drought-ridden areas east of the Cascade Mountains. Google engineers have also been meeting with representatives from countries in Africa's Congo River Basin to see if some of the moisture from their rainforest could be blown away and aimed at the Sahara Desert.

Not everyone is thrilled about these ideas, however. Environmentalist groups warn that interfering with weather patterns and climates—even on a small scale—could have unforeseen consequences. They're worried what might happen to plants and animals living in those areas, and are urging Google and local governments to proceed with great caution. Others are concerned that being able to control the weather gives Google

Maybe there will be more rainbows, too?

too much power: What if they decide to start charging people for favorable weather, or choose to restrict access for reasons all their own? Still others worry that growing too dependent on the system could lead to big trouble down the road if it ever happened to fail.

It's hard to say at this point where exactly this new technology will end up or how it will all turn out. Still, one thing is for sure: the residents of Holland couldn't be happier . . . now that they've learned how to apply sunscreen, anyway.

Talk It Out: Humans versus Nature

Human beings have always changed the environment. On a small scale—like cutting down a tree or building a campfire—nature can bounce back without any major problems. The more of us there are and the more technology we have, however, the greater chance we might cause serious trouble. Many people worry that advances like genetic engineering and nuclear power will cause far more harm than good. Others argue that those very same discoveries and inventions will allow more and more people to continue to thrive on Earth.

What do you think? How should we decide which technologies are worth pursuing and which should be halted? How can countries work together to ensure the safety of their own citizens as well as others around the world? Are humankind's continuing scientific inventions and discoveries nudging us toward a brighter future . . . or pushing us to doom and destruction? There are no easy answers, but thinking about the issues and sharing your thoughts with others—as well as listening to their views in return—is an important first step toward growing our awareness and understanding, as well as caring for our planet.

FIRENADO!

A wildfire, on its own, can be devastating. Combine one with a tornado, however, and you've got a surefire recipe for disaster. Unfortunately, this combination is much more common than you might expect.

Why? Believe it or not, fire can actually *create* whirlwinds that look a lot like tornadoes. Most of the time, these "tornadoes" are actually what are known as fire whirls: columns of rotating air and flames rising up from the ground. They're similar to the small whirlwinds or dust devils you might see swirling leaves above warm pavement or spinning sand in a dry field. As hot air rises, it pulls in more hot air behind it. The column of air starts to swirl and— WHOOSH . . . instant whirlwind. But when a fire causes a whirlwind, it becomes a spinning **vortex** of flame.

A fire whirl in action

But wait . . . it gets worse.

Really big fires, like wildfires, can also make full-blown and very real tornadoes. Here's how it works. Wildfires generate a whole lot of warm air. The burning plants release

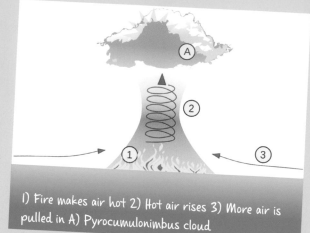

1) Fire makes air hot 2) Hot air rises 3) More air is pulled in A) Pyrocumulonimbus cloud

moisture, so the warm air is mixed with water vapor. The moist, warm air rises and eventually cools high in the atmosphere. When it cools, the water **condenses** quickly into a dark, massive, terrifying cloud formation called a pyrocumulonimbus. Basically, an instant thunderstorm in an otherwise blue sky.

Now, that might sound quite handy: Maybe the rain from a massive thunderstorm could help snuff out the wildfire, right? Not *these* thunderstorms. The rain might evaporate before ever falling to the ground. The winds caused by the storm could cause the fire to spread

vortex: A whirling mass of air that pulls things toward its center

condense: Change from a gas into a liquid

faster or in unexpected directions. Lightning could occur, possibly sparking even more fires. And thunderstorms can also produce— you guessed it—honest-to-goodness tornadoes: spinning vortices of air coming down from the clouds toward the Earth. Those tornadoes can be even more dangerous than normal. In addition to their destructive wind power, they can also carry burning embers that end up spreading the fire farther, faster, and even more unpredictably than before.

The danger likely won't be limited to the area affected by the firestorm itself, either. The smoke that gets pulled up into the atmosphere releases particles of ash and soot as high as ten miles up. The particles drift along with air currents to other parts of the world, just like normal clouds but with a nasty punch. Wherever

Try It: Make Your Own Cloud

Wouldn't it be great if YOU could control the weather? Here's a little science fun that gives you the power to make your own (tiny) cloud. First, round up your supplies. You'll need a large glass jar with a lid, hot water, ice, and an aerosol spray can (like hairspray or air freshener). Then, follow these steps:

1. Pour hot (but not boiling) water into the jar. (Add some food coloring if you want.) Swirl it around to warm up the glass.

2. Place the lid upside down on top of the jar and fill the lid with ice cubes. Wait about thirty seconds.

3. Quickly lift off the lid, spray the aerosol inside the jar, and put the upside-down lid full of ice back on top.

4. Watch your cloud grow and swirl inside the jar! Whenever you're ready, lift off the lid and let your cloud escape.

How does it work? The warm, moist air rises to the top, where it meets the air cooled by the ice cubes in the lid. When the aerosol spray is added, the cooled water vapor condenses onto the particles to form the cloud.

the ash and soot ends up coming down, air and water quality suffer and ice and snow may melt faster. That's bad news for crops, wildlife, and—of course—people.

Scientists are now able to track these ash clouds as well as predict their behavior in an effort to minimize the danger. Unfortunately, this work is likely to become more and more important in the coming years. Global climate change will bring warmer temperatures, less moisture, and increased winds to certain areas—all of which will lead to even bigger, badder, faster wildfires. And those fires, and the clouds they create, could in turn contribute to even more climate change. Scientists aren't sure of all the implications here yet, but it's clear we still have a lot to learn about fire, fire whirls, and firestorms.

YOU'VE JUST READ ABOUT *a volcanic eruption that made the loudest sound ever heard by humans, a plan to harness the power of internet-connected windmills to create better weather, and tornadoes created by wildfires. Do you think you know which one of these surprising stories isn't true? Go find out if you're correct!*

PART 2

SenSational SCienCe

Now we're going to kick things up a notch
and take a closer look at some specific branches
of science. Chemistry is all about how various
substances in our world interact with one another.
Physics deals with energy, forces, and movement. And, of
course, you can learn lots of fascinating things about space by
studying astronomy. But remember, not all of the following stories
are true. You've been warned!

A. QUITE A SWEET STORY!

For most of you, a glass of water is probably nothing special. Feeling thirsty? You simply turn on your kitchen faucet, or put a glass under your water filter, or get a bottle from the fridge.

But many folks around the world are not so lucky. By current estimates, 844 million people—that's one out of every

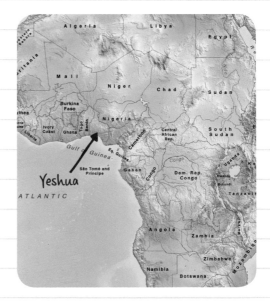

Yeshua

nine people alive right now!—do not have access to clean drinking water.

A number of international organizations around the world are working to help address this crisis, much of which is centered in **rural** towns and villages. One of these organizations, Oxfam, has launched a program to help villagers build their own safe **wells**. As you might imagine, this has had many great benefits—including one that was *extremely* unexpected!

Residents in the village of Yeshua, in the Ibadan region of southwest Nigeria, have long relied on surface water

rural: In the countryside, not in towns or cities

well: A deep hole dug in the earth to reach drinking water

Heave, ho!
Making a well!

(from rivers and lakes) to meet their drinking and personal hygiene needs. But impure water can carry serious health risks, including typhoid fever, cholera, and more. And so in early 2014, enterprising villagers set to work installing a well for the use of the whole village.

Once it was complete, the well delivered a flow of water from deep in the earth that was just as clean and clear as expected. But after a few days passed, drinkers began to notice something curious about the water: It tasted . . . sweet?! Some even described a slight fizz in the water.

Was this water—or soda?

Confused about what was going on, villagers closed off the

well. But over the following days, each early morning found the well partly uncovered, having clearly been used in the night. Young villagers, it turned out, could not get enough of this sweet natural flow, and were bypassing the ban to sneak in and drink their fill in the dead of night.

Clearly, it was time to bring in the safety experts. Tests were run. And the verdict? The well's water did indeed run sweet, and for a most unexpected reason. Nigeria is the fourth biggest producer of papayas in the world, and the village of Yeshua lies just outside one of the country's largest farms. It seems that tons of overripe fruit from the farm were being disposed of in large pits not far from the village. Over time, runoff from the fermented fruit made its way into the water deep below the soil—resulting in an unexpectedly sweet, improbably healthy soda fountain with a hint of natural fizz.

Now, hold up just a minute. Did we just say *healthy*?

We did indeed. Experts not only judged Yeshua's well water safe to drink, but were surprised to discover how beneficial it was. A natural superfruit, papaya is loaded with **antioxidants**, essential vitamins and nutrients, and is even thought to have cancer-fighting properties. And a vast majority of the health benefits contained in the fruit transferred right over into the well's water, resulting in something like commercially sold "kefir water" that is so prized for its **probiotic** qualities.

That's a lot of thirsty people

So that sweet soda spout? *Even better for you than a glass of water!*

As you might imagine, Yeshua has been flooded with companies wanting to bottle and sell from their sweet source. But so far, the village has said a firm "no thanks" to any grand-scale plans. "This is our home," said village elder Adaobi Eze. "We have been given this gift and for now, that is enough." The famed well has resulted in an uptick of travelers and tourists to the area, and Yeshuans are more than willing to share a cup with any thirsty traveler.

antioxidant: A natural substance that promotes good health

probiotic: Something that helps keep the digestive system healthy

Which all goes to show that you never can tell what lies below the surface of something. Do a little digging, and you may be surprised at what you find!

Try It: How Sweet Is YOUR Drink?

Most of us like a sweet drink now and then, but do we know how much sugar we're getting when we take a sip? Here's one way to help you visualize what you're actually drinking.

1. First, collect some of your favorite drinks: milk, juice, soda, water. Write the name of each beverage at the top of its own sheet of colored paper.

2. Next, read the nutrition labels for each drink. Below each beverage name, write down how many grams of sugar are in a single serving of the drink.

3. Now, get some sugar and a teaspoon from the kitchen. Four grams of sugar is about the same as one teaspoon of granulated sugar. Measure how much sugar is in each drink and place it on the appropriate paper.

Are you surprised at the results? Is the amount of sugar in different drinks more or less than you expected?

According to the American Heart Association, sugary drinks are the largest single source of calories in most people's diets, with the average American taking in about 39 pounds of sugar each year just from our beverages! Unfortunately, just one sugary drink per day increases your risk of diseases like obesity, diabetes, heart disease, and cancer. Kids should have no more than three teaspoons (12 grams) of sugar per day. Are you getting more than that? If so, perhaps it's time to rethink your drink!

HERE BE GIANTS

When you think of crystals, what comes to mind? Diamonds, salt, snowflakes? In any case, they're usually fairly small, right? Well, that is *not* the case with the crystals we're going to talk about today. *These* gigantic crystals are the largest ever to be found on Earth: as big as telephone poles!

In April 2000, miners discovered the Cave of Crystals 1,000 feet below the ground under Naica Mountain in Chihuahua, Mexico. They were drilling a new tunnel in hopes of expanding the mine.

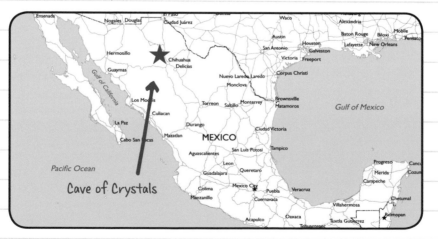

Cave of Crystals

The area had previously been flooded with groundwater, but the mine operators had set up pumps to drain it away. Eloy Delgado was one of the first people to ever see the forest of huge **selenite** crystals. "It was beautiful," he told *Smithsonian Magazine*, "like light reflecting off a broken mirror."

But he couldn't stick around to admire them for very long. While the crystals might look a bit like ice, the temperature in the cave is *hot*—it can reach up to 136 degrees Fahrenheit! In fact, some visitors have nearly died from heatstroke, and there's so much moisture in the air that it can fill up your lungs and drown you in minutes.

Despite the risks, scientists have been drawn to explore the cavern and its wonders. Geologists were stunned by both the size and purity of the crystals, and Dr. Juan Manuel García-Ruiz, from the University of Granada, in Spain, made repeated trips into the dangerous cave in hopes of discovering how and when they were formed. He collected tiny pockets of liquid that were trapped inside the crystals, then took them back to his lab and conducted tests and experiments.

What did he learn? The crystals formed because they were surrounded by water rich in minerals and kept at a fairly constant, warm temperature over thousands of years. The key to their enormous size, perhaps surprisingly, was that they grew very slowly. In fact, García-Ruiz calculated that to get as large as they are now, they must have been growing undisturbed for around 500,000 years!

selenite: A colorless, transparent form of the mineral gypsum

Other scientists are also interested in the cave . . . and its inhabitants. That's right: it's not just crystals down there. Dr. Penelope Boston, director of the Astrobiology Institute at NASA, studies unusual life-forms in extreme environments here

Beams of selenite inside the Cave of Crystals

Special containment suits allowed more time in the cave

on Earth to learn about what life might look like on other planets. Like García-Ruiz, she risked the heat of the cavern to collect fluid from inside the crystals, but she was looking for something much different.

And she found it. She was able to identify—and revive—forty different strains of microbes, and even some viruses. They're

Our Weird Earth

Earth science is always fascinating, often surprising, and sometimes can seem completely bonkers. Check out these ten fabulous-and-all-real natural science marvels—well, nine real marvels plus one fake! But which is which?

1. SKYPUNCH: Also known as a fallstreak hole or a hole-punch cloud, this is when a portion of a cloud freezes over; with just the right conditions, a hole drops out of its center, leaving a big gap.

2. STEVE: The name given to a newly discovered atmospheric phenomenon in the shape of a purple ribbon of light (rather than the usual oval or curtain shape).

3. PENITENTES: Spiky ice spears that can grow as high as 13 feet, formed under certain conditions when snow is converted straight to vapor, without melting first.

4. BALL LIGHTNING: Unexplained phenomenon that looks like a wide pocket of electricity, lasting longer than a lightning bolt and often exploding.

5. PELE'S HAIR: Thin golden strands of lava named after a Hawaiian volcano goddess, formed when drops of lava are caught by the wind, pulled, and stretched out before they cool.

(Continued on next page)

Our Weird Earth (continued)

6. SNOW DOUGHNUTS: Also known as snow rollers, this rare phenomenon occurs when chunks of snow gather into a wheel shape and roll downhill.

7. BRINICLES: Thin columns of frozen seawater that form under sheets of ice, centering around very cold streams of water.

8. GLASS BEETLES: Small glass balls formed when extra-hot conditions fuse the desert sand into glass, trapping tiny insects at their center.

9. FROZEN METHANE BUBBLES: Frozen gas bubbles in some high-altitude lakes. The ice disks bubble and fizz when the melt begins—and are flammable!

10. LIGHT PILLARS: Thin, colorful columns of light stretching up from around cities during certain extra-cold weather conditions.

different from anything scientists had ever seen, and they're estimated to be around 50,000 years old.

Alas, we may not be hearing more discoveries about the Cave of Crystals anytime soon. Since its operations there have finished, the mining company has turned off the pumps and allowed water to once again flood the chamber. That's bad news for scientists, who can no longer study the crystals. But it's good news for the crystals themselves, which can go back to growing, ever so slowly, deep below the surface, with no one around to bother them.

Let's check back on them in another 500,000 years or so, shall we?

ARE YOU BOARED YET?

If you aren't boared, then keep reading. Because this story has it all: disasters, explosions, and . . . BOARS! Yep, that's one subject that is never boaring. Er, *boring*. Let's get back to the subject at hand.

The boars we're going to examine today are no laughing matter. In the last couple of years, farmers in northern Japan have noticed an increase in the local wild boar population. These aggressive,

fearless creatures are venturing down from the mountains and wreaking havoc in farms and gardens. But the creepiest thing about these boars? They are **radioactive**.

Yep, you read that right. But let's skip back

CAUTION: RADIOACTIVE (and it bites!)

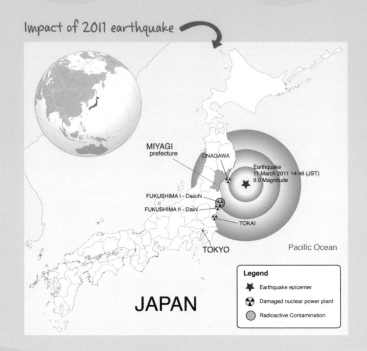

Impact of 2011 earthquake

MIYAGI
prefecture
ONAGAWA

Earthquake
11 March 2011 14:46 (JST)
9.0 Magnitude

FUKUSHIMA I - Daiichi
&
FUKUSHIMA II - Daini

TOKAI

TOKYO

Pacific Ocean

Legend

★ Earthquake epicenter

☢ Damaged nuclear power plant

⬤ Radioactive Contamination

JAPAN

in time a little, to see how it all began.

Before the boars, before the explosion, before the tsunami, there was an earthquake. In the sleepy postnoon hours of March 11, 2011, a 9.0 magnitude tremor shook the northeast coast of Japan. It was not only the strongest earthquake to hit Japan, but the fourth largest quake on record *in the entire world*! Tragically, over 15,000 people were killed in this disaster. But that was not the end of the awful repercussions.

The earthquake was so strong that it physically shifted parts of the Japanese mainland about ten feet into the ocean. This disruption caused enormous ocean swells known as tsunamis, which pounded the country's coastlines.

radioactive: Containing particles of nuclear radiation

Among the sites impacted by the tsunami was a **nuclear power plant** in Fukushima, where flooding caused an explosion and meltdown of three of the six **reactors**—pushing huge amounts of deadly radiation out into the air. Nearby towns were quickly evacuated, and some of these ghost towns remain empty to this day.

Empty, that is . . . except for the boars.

Formerly reclusive mountain-dwellers, wild boars have been flocking to the abandoned towns around Fukushima, perhaps drawn by the uninhabited, food-rich landscape. But much of the flora and forage in the area is still dangerously radioactive—in particular, a favorite food of the boars: wild mushrooms, which draw their nourishment from the radiation-tainted soil.

Satellite view of the Fukushima reactor three minutes after the second explosion

nuclear power plant: Factory that converts nuclear energy into power for everyday use

reactor: Structure made to safely create and control nuclear energy

The boars continue to grow and multiply, yet they've shown no ill effects from their high-**isotope** diet. In the past, hunters might have trapped the boars to feed their families, as boar is considered a local delicacy. But radioactivity levels in the meat are now too high for human consumption. And with their greater numbers, the boars are now growing more aggressive, threatening locals and making resettlement tough in some places—even after the environmental danger has passed.

isotope: The radioactive form of an element

What's next? So far, no boars have developed superpowers (that we know of). But the whole situation is an interesting object lesson in cause and effect—how every element in the natural world is linked, and how one event can have far-reaching implications, well beyond the initial impact.

Bags and bags of radioactive waste ☹

Talk It Out: I Cause, You Effect

It's a pretty basic principle: for each action, there is a reaction. Just about every change has an effect on the environment and the lives of those around it. Examining and discussing things that have or might have occurred can be both interesting and instructive.

Think about a significant change that has recently happened in your home, school, or neighborhood—such as changing up one of the rooms in your house, or getting a new school principal, or seeing an old parking lot being turned into a playground.

Choose one of those changes, and brainstorm what effects it has had. See if you can break down the results, step-by-step. Now analyze them: Has the overall effect been positive or negative? Is it possible that sometimes a positive change can have a negative effect, or the other way around? How can thinking about cause and effect shape your actions and decision-making in the future?

IN THIS CHAPTER YOU *discovered a sweet surprise welling up from the ground, an underground cave of gigantic crystals, and some dangerously radioactive wild boars. Which one of these stories isn't true? Are you sure? Better be careful! It might not be the one you think it is. . . .*

A. THE BEESTS ON THE BEACH

It's a breezy, blue-sky day in Ipswich, Massachusetts, in the summer of 2015. You're out for a walk on Crane Beach with your family. Up ahead, a crowd has gathered. They're all staring at something: a creature that's big and sticklike and billowing—all at once. Something that strides confidently across the sand on multiple **revolving** legs, tossing up sand as it goes, with several people keeping pace.

Is it an alien come aground? Some enormous stick

A Strandbeest in the Netherlands

insect? A new type of vehicle, maybe?

None of that. What you have stumbled upon, you lucky beach-walker, is a Strandbeest. Brainchild of the Dutch artist and inventor Theo Jansen, the Strandbeest phenomenon has swept across the world in recent years—from Delft to Okinawa to Lima to Madrid, and many more cities all across the globe.

But what *are* Strandbeests? Let's first take a closer look at their quirky **engineer**.

Since his youth, Theo Jansen has always been creating. He once constructed and launched a 15-foot, **helium**-filled flying saucer that was believable enough to throw onlookers into a full-blown panic about a feared alien invasion. But over the years, Jansen's dreams turned

revolving: Turning over and over

engineer: Someone who designs or builds machines and other structures

to robots. And not just any robots. "When the weather was beautiful I thought it was a waste of time to sit in front of the computer," Jansen told the Danish news source *Artificial*. So he conceived of an entirely new type of self-powered, environmentally friendly robot, a creature of humble construction and artistic design.

In a world where inventions seem to grow more technical and technological every day, Strandbeests stand in sharp contrast: they are powered by nothing but wind. Jansen wanted to create a robot that could be one with nature, that could both draw from the natural world and give back to it in kind.

Jansen began creating his Strandbeest in 1990, in what was meant to be a one-year project. He's *still* hard at work on them today. And no wonder! These **kinetic** sculptures—created from plastic PVC piping, wood, and fabric— have an allure that is undeniable and irresistible. They might not be true artificial intelligence (yet!), but with the right conditions they can move fully on their own, reacting with their environment in authentic and free-spirited ways. If they move too close

Who goes there?!

to the waves, for example, the beests are able to sidestep back to avoid the water and carry on with their beach stroll unimpeded. They can also store up small amounts of wind power, for seamless continuous mobility even if the breeze dies down.

So, what's next for the Strandbeest? For now, Jansen tours the world with his creations, displaying them on beaches or in museums to masses of eager spectators. Just like that crowd you found on the beach, hundreds and thousands of art and nature lovers across the globe gather for Jansen's demonstrations. But, if you ask him, this is only the beginning. Jansen is constantly improving his design, and he envisions a day when Strandbeests roam the beaches entirely under their own power. "They should survive on their own in the future," he said in a 2007 TED talk, "learning to live on their own." These future beachcombers would protect and regenerate the landscape, tossing and shifting sand up the beach to protect against erosion, as fully self-sustaining, independent creatures.

kinetic: To do with movement

Theo Jansen with one of his "beests"

So if you're strolling down the beach on some future windswept day and you see in the distance a lumbering, gawky, beanpole contraption coming toward you with a stick-arm raised in friendly greeting . . . remember, it just might be the first of a whole new type of artificial life.

Try It: Make Your Own Minibeest

"The real ideas," Jansen told the *New Yorker*, "come about by chance." What might you invent completely by chance? Your mission, should you choose to accept it: create your own miniature creature. Start by collecting as many different types of materials as you can find. They could be anything that inspires you—anything at all! For example:

* pipe cleaners
* flexible wiring
* duct tape
* empty plastic bottles
* empty thread spools
* cloth squares

Now look over your haul. Lay it all out in front of you. Move things around: stack, switch, rummage. What fits? What goes well together? What makes an interesting contrast? What connects?

And then . . . How might you bring it all together? What kind of creature will you create? What could it do? And—just as important—what will you call it?

B. FIDGET SPINNERS' REVENGE

Ah, fidget spinners. You know . . . those strangely satisfying little toys with the disc in the middle that you can hold on to while you spin the "arms" around and around . . . and around and around and around. They were designed to help people focus better by giving them something to do with their hands, but they ended up causing a fair amount of distraction, too. In some cases, they even caused injuries.

Whether you view them as handy helpers, a fun fad, or an outright

"Spin on!"

annoyance, those addictive little devices were everywhere for a while. Despite all the controversy, though, they were pretty harmless . . . right?

Maybe not.

Scientists say that it's a good thing the fidget spinner fad didn't grow any more popular than it did, because things could have gotten way out of control. In fact, some experts believe that we narrowly avoided disaster—on a planetary scale.

Hold on. Planetary disaster . . . from fidget spinners?

You read that right. It all comes down to physics—in particular, to gravity: the force that causes objects to fall toward the center of the Earth and keeps the Earth orbiting around the sun. But what does that have to do with fidget spinners, you ask? We're so glad you did. Be warned, however: The answer might make your head spin!

Physicist Michael Taylor of the Denver Institute of Science studied fidget spinners

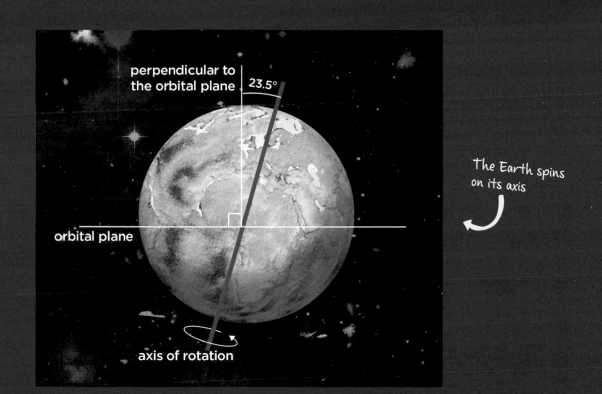

perpendicular to
the orbital plane   23.5°

orbital plane

axis of rotation

The Earth spins
on its axis

in his lab. He and his team confirmed that the circular motion
of every fidget spinner creates its own tiny—but measurable—
gravitational force. That's no big deal, of course, when there's
just one of the little gadgets, or even a few. But if you were to get
thousands of them together, in one place . . . the consequences
could be devastating. "Added together," Taylor says, "it's entirely
possible that something in the realm of ten to twelve thousand
fidget spinners, spinning simultaneously in close proximity to one
another, could create enough gravitational force to affect us on a
global scale."

You see, the Earth's center of gravity is not as fixed and stable as most of us might think—it is surprisingly susceptible to outside forces. There aren't many unexpected gravitational forces on our planet, so there's usually nothing to worry about. But if we were to put too many fidget spinners too close together and they just happened to all be spinning in the same direction (even for a few seconds!) . . . this could conceivably create enough gravitational force to mess up the Earth's gravitational fields, or even alter our planet's orbit around the sun.

That realization worries Taylor, who has asked the folks at Guinness World Records to disqualify any entries involving the

Talk It Out: And the World Record Goes to . . . YOU!

Don't you love reading about the impressive, crazy, and sometimes just plain weird things people have done to get their names listed in the books of Guinness World Records? Balancing the most scoops of ice cream on a single cone, for example (123 scoops). Or growing the longest fingernails (combined length: 29 feet, 8 inches).

If you were going to try to set a world record, what would you do? How would you prepare? Who would help you? Do you think you would be successful? Discuss your ideas, your plans . . . and their potential consequences.

User beware!

toys. "I think it's not likely that thousands of people with fidget spinners would gather in one place," Taylor says, "but you never know what people will try, especially to achieve some sort of brand-new world record." And we certainly can't afford to find out. Can you imagine how even the slightest change in gravity would affect your most basic activities, like jumping or playing soccer? How about more serious things, like flying in an airplane or designing a bridge? And even the slightest change in our planet's orbit would wreak havoc on our seasons, climate, and food supply.

So go ahead and play with your fidget spinner as much as you want . . . just don't invite thousands of friends to join you, okay?

C. ANY BODY CAN LIVE FOREVER!

All right, before you get too excited about this story title, we should probably get something straight. There is a very fine difference between "anybody" and "any *body*." And it is the latter we are talking about today—the human body. Part of it, anyway.

According to an old saying, there are two things you can be absolutely sure of in life: (1) You will be born. (2) At some point—hopefully after a good long time—you will die. But what, dare I ask, do you think happens *after* you die?

Now, there are spiritual and **metaphysical** answers to that question, and people all across the world have different views and beliefs . . . none of which we are going to ponder here. No, today we're going to talk about what happens *to the body* after death.

> **metaphysical:** Having to do with the mind or spirit instead of the physical body

Burial, you say? Or maybe **cremation**?

Those are good options. But you might be surprised to know

that these are not the only **postmortem** possibilities: just ask the people at a company called LifeGem, whose goal is to make sure that your loved one can stick around with you indefinitely—in some form, that is.

In a pretty unusual form. (Might we say, a *brilliant* one?)

It starts with a smattering of science—specifically, the science of diamonds. At the molecular level, a diamond is nothing more than a collection of common carbon atoms—organized in a certain way through extreme heat and pressure, a process that occurs naturally over many years. LifeGem starts with this principle, and then takes it quite a bit further. They begin with the cremated remains of your loved one. From these ashes, the company extracts a quantity of carbon, which is then converted to graphite. This graphite is placed within their special "diamond press." Can you guess what happens next?

cremation: Reducing a dead body to ashes by burning it

postmortem: After death

Yep. From this matter, a diamond is made.

Next LifeGem cuts, sets, and mounts this very precious stone

This diamond is not your relative. But it could be!

and delivers it to the customer. Your loved one has become one of the most precious substances on Earth—and can now be mounted onto a brooch, ring, or pendant, to be carried with you wherever you go.

We get that this idea might send a lot of people running for the door. Others might see it as an excellent story starter and may be sharpening their fiction pencils as we speak. But many have found great comfort in knowing that, through this innovative process, some part of their beloved can remain close to their heart.

And that's not the only option. There is also a whole fleet of "**green** burial" options like this one. Supporters of

Amazing After-Death Doings

These are all actual things that people have done with their relatives' remains (many at the request of the deceased)—all but one, that is. Can you sort through these wacky wishes and find the fake?

1. Frisbee inventor Ed Headrick asked that his remains be molded into "memorial flying discs" to be passed out to family members.

2. Fredric J. Baur, designer of the Pringles can, asked that his ashes be laid to rest inside one of his iconic creations.

3. Gene Roddenberry, creator of the Star Trek series, had his ashes launched into deep space.

4. Edgar Allan Poe took the death of his young wife so hard that he kept her remains in a small snuffbox that he carried with him everywhere he went.

5. Author Hunter S. Thompson's ashes were shot out of a cannon from a 150-foot tower, while his favorite music was played nearby.

(Continued on next page)

6. Country music legend Jimmy Dean was buried in a custom-made, $350,000 mausoleum shaped like a grand piano.

7. Tupac Shakur's ashes were smoked by his rapper friends.

8. Dayna D., a woman from Alaska, reported to *Inked* magazine that she used the ashes from her daughter's remains as part of a memorial tattoo on her wrist.

9. John Lennon's ashes were scattered in New York City's Central Park.

10. Political activist Joe Hill's ashes were sealed into 600 envelopes and mailed to like-minded recipients.

green: Able to be recycled, contributing to the Earth's health

London Necropolis Railway: See *Two Truths and a Lie: Histories and Mysteries*, page 21

biodegradable: Something that breaks down naturally in the earth

these methods point to the destructive impact that metal caskets, concrete vaults, or chemical embalming fluids have on the Earth. There's also the space taken up by cemeteries and burial plots: with world population at an all-time high, the demand will only grow. (And the **London Necropolis Railway**, as we know, is no longer in service.)

So, several companies have created **biodegradable** receptacles in which to deposit remains. Options include an egg-shaped pod, a decorative urn, or a handy indoor planter pot. Into these you place your loved one's ashes combined

That's one keepsake that will never fade

Capsula Mundi, an egg-shaped, biodegradable, organic casket

with a rich soil mixture, add a seed or a plant—and the new growth process begins. I mean, we honor our loved ones with stones in a graveyard . . . why not with a living, growing tree?

As you can see, body recycling is rapidly becoming a postmortem potluck of green, clean options. After all, isn't that what we all hope for on some level: a way to capture and hold just a bit more of those we love? They live on forever within our hearts already; now there are some surprising new ways they can linger outside it, too.

IN THIS CHAPTER WE *have been introduced to a group of beachcombing automatons, learned about the perils of fidget spinners, and been instructed in a variety of options for after-death preservation. Of course, one of these scintillating selections is entirely untrue. But which one? Dig, discuss . . . dive on in!*

A. HELLO, GOODBYE, WHOOSH!

One great thing about science fiction is that it can give you a great sense of cool stuff that isn't quite—but *should be*—possible, and that really might be someday. In fact, quite a few inventions were described by science fiction authors well before being made in real life.

(For instance, Jules Verne and the submarine, or William Gibson and the internet.) And one spiffy invention that comes up a lot in science fiction is teleportation.

What *is* teleportation? We are so glad you asked.

A teleportation device is usually a door or portal you can step through (or put stuff into—for example, a cake!). And then it's: Goodbye, New York . . . *whoosh* . . . Hello, Shanghai. That's it! Blink of an eye and you are (or your sweet treat is) halfway around the world, neat as you please.

Science fiction, right?

Not so fast. In July 2017, the scientific community saw an incredible breakthrough: Chinese scientist Ji-Gang Ren and his colleagues from the University of Science and Technology of China, set a new record by teleporting particles of information

The Micius satellite and three cooperating ground stations

from a ground base in Tibet clear up to the Micius satellite **orbiting** hundreds of miles above the Earth. To do so, they used a wildly cool principle called entanglement, whereby two different bits of **matter** (even ones that might be far apart) become tangled up together, so that their information merges and they act as one unit. Amazing!

Early seeds of this type of teleportation date back to the 1990s, when breakthroughs in **quantum mechanics** laid the foundation for this instant

orbiting: Moving around a planet, star, or moon

matter: Any physical stuff that takes up space and has mass

quantum mechanics: A type of physics that deals with the tiny elements that make up our universe

transfer of information from one spot to another. And the principles of entanglement go back even further, famously referred to by Albert Einstein in the 1930s as "spooky action at a distance." So stuff like this had been done before, but on a very small scale and from quite close at hand. This new breakthrough shattered all previous records, in terms of distance *and* reliability.

But what does it mean to say that "information" is being teleported? It means the state of one particle gets communicated to another particle. It's not exactly like a physical object getting sent somewhere, but more like a change happening to a matching object at a distance.

Imagine two particles, a galaxy apart. One turns into a basketball. Now, on the other side of a galaxy—POOF!—there's also a basketball!

Scientists haven't yet been able to do that, but they can get matching information to pop up in another place, which is a massively cool step. The transfer of information has been a driving force behind human history, and every time an invention comes along to make it happen faster, the world changes all over again: the written word, the printing press, the telephone, the internet. Just think about how people kept in touch 50 or 100 years ago. It was . . . a *lot* slower!

Here on planet Earth, we can now almost instantly send messages to one another. But what about across space? That's a whole different thing. Sending a message to the spacecraft that scientists have sent out into our solar system can take minutes, hours, or even *days*. What if we could

Take a Count of This!

Measuring stuff—it's pretty basic, right? Usually we're talking about things like miles or gallons or pounds. Ordinary terms most of us know well. But here are some terms of measurement that are *not* ordinary at all. Check out these outlandish counting or measuring terms and you'll see what we mean! Just remember, one of them comes straight from our imagination. . . .

1. SMIDGEN: exactly half a pinch, or 1/32 of a teaspoon

2. PORONKUSEMA: in Finland, the distance a reindeer can travel before having to stop and go pee

3. HAND: for measuring horses, equal to four inches (originally a hand's span from thumb to little finger)

4. MICKEY: named for the iconic Disney character, the tiniest space a computer mouse can move, or about 0.1 mm

5. SNEEZE EFFECT: a casual way to measure pollen in the air, related to how many times a seasonal allergy sufferer sneezes in a row

6. WAFFLE HOUSE INDEX: informal government measurement for how bad a natural disaster is (whether Waffle House restaurants in the area are open)

(Continued on next page)

Take a Count of This! (continued)

7. JIFFY: a way to measure time, equivalent to how long it takes light to travel one centimeter in a vacuum

8. BEARD-SECOND: how long an average beard will grow in a given second (about five nanometers, or five billionths of a meter)

9. GOOGOL: the second-largest number that has been named, written 10^{100}, or 1 followed by 100 zeroes

10. GOOGOLPLEX: the largest named number: 1 with googol zeroes following it

instantly send information across the farthest reaches of the galaxy, even to the most faraway planets? That, my friends, is the kind of thing that keeps scientists up at night.

So the future of teleportation winds on. There hasn't yet been any movement of people or physical objects (not even cake, sadly). But this

The antennae used to transmit the quantum information

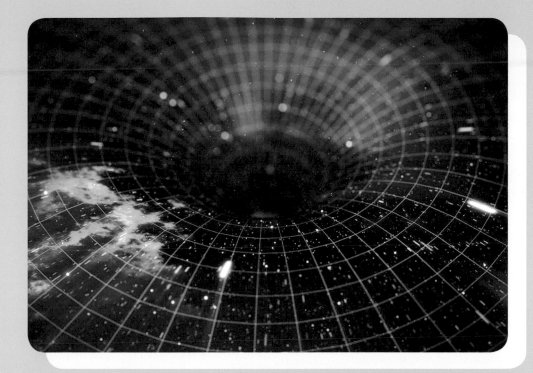

new breakthrough, thanks to the power of quantum mechanics, is a good step in that direction. This author, for one, can totally envision a time when somebody can pop into a portal on one side of the world and, quick as a blink, end up clear across the world—or maybe in outer space.

Our science fictional future may be just around the corner. Get ready for it!

B. THINGS YOU THINK ABOUT WHEN THE SKY IS FALLING

Some days are pretty ordinary, ho-hum, just like all the rest. There are a *lot* of those days. But then there are other days that are . . . less normal. For example, the day enjoyed by an Alabama woman named Ann Hodges on November 30, 1954.

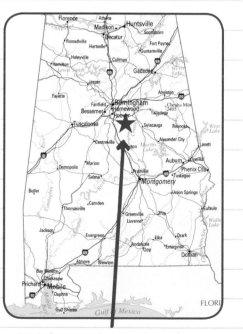

Ann's home in Oak Grove, Alabama

Just another Tuesday. That's what Ann might have been thinking as she went about her morning. Maybe she cleaned the house a bit, or weeded her garden, or read a book. Sometime after lunch, she lay down for a nap on the couch. The house was quiet. But then suddenly . . .

BAM!

There's a horrible crashing sound. She looks up and there's a hole in her ceiling! Her radio appears to have exploded! And—OUCH!—there's an agonizing pain in her hip. What is going on?

At first, Ann might have thought there had been some kind of explosion. But then she

carom: Hit and bounce off

saw, on the floor near her, a dark chunk of stone about the size of a loaf of bread. And the hole above it went clear through to the outside! Had this rock smashed through her roof, torn a hole in her living room ceiling, **caromed** off her radio cabinet, then crashed into her hip?

Yes, yes, yes, and yes.

Here's what took this day straight into the history books: Ann Hodges was the first and only human in recorded history to be hit by a meteorite falling from space.

Yep. An 8.5-pound rock was catapulted down from outer

It was a very confusing day

space—way up among the planets and asteroids in our solar system—to dive-bomb an unsuspecting lady in her living room.

Now let's take a moment to explain some lingo: A meteoroid is a chunk of rock or **debris** floating out in space. When a meteoroid enters Earth's **atmosphere**, it usually burns up in a flash of light known as a "shooting star" or meteor. And any plucky pebble that manages to make its way safely through the atmosphere and reach the Earth's surface? It then gets dubbed a meteorite. And if it hits a woman named Ann Hodges, it might get an even more specific name: the Hodges meteorite.

debris: Useless or discarded material

atmosphere: Layer of gas that surrounds and protects a planet

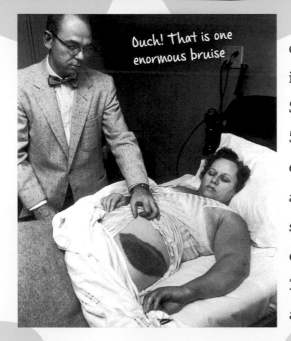

Ouch! That is one enormous bruise

As you might imagine, outer space is full of rocks and other debris, and a fair bit of this makes it into our atmosphere. The Planetary Science Institute estimates that about 500 meteorites hit Earth's surface every year, but most are tiny. There are exceptions: In 2009, a meteorite smashed through the windshield of an SUV in Ontario, Canada. In 2013, an enormous meteor (as big as a six-story building!) entered

The actual meteorite that hit Ann Hodges!

Earth's atmosphere over Russia, exploding into fragments just 15 miles above the surface, creating many smaller meteorites that landed nearby. But these are the exceptions; 90–95% of all meteoroids burn right up on entering Earth's atmosphere.

With so few dropping in to say hello, meteorite fragments tend to be valuable. A nearby farmer found a separate piece of the Hodges meteorite and sold it for enough money to buy a small house and a car. Ann Hodges was not so lucky. She

What Else Is Falling from the Sky?

The Hodges meteorite might be the only rock from space to hit a person, but it's far from the only strange object to rain down from the sky and cause a stir. Check out this list of weird, wacky, and unbelievable visitors from the air up there. Just remember that one of these is made up . . .

1. A chunk of frozen pee (believed to be from a passing airplane) crashed through a woman's ceiling, hitting her on the shoulder. (2016)

2. A small town in Kentucky was pelted with meat chunks from the sky, eventually thought to have been vomited by carrion birds. (1876)

3. A region in Australia was showered with millions of spiders falling from the sky and traveling on air currents. (2015)

4. Hungry beachgoers in southern France were delighted when hundreds of macaron cookies hailed down one afternoon—a nearby overturned transport truck and a lucky gust were the cause. (1986)

5. A puppy fell from the sky into a woman's California yard (apparently dropped by a hawk); she kept him and named him TJ Heavenly. (2012)

(Continued on next page)

What Else Is Falling from the Sky? (continued)

6. Reports of fish showers are fairly common in some parts of the world—one town in Honduras has a yearly festival to celebrate the phenomenon.

7. Residents of a South Carolina town were alarmed by white powder repeatedly showering down on them; it was found to be nondairy creamer blown from a nearby factory. (1969)

8. A man fishing off the Falkland Islands was knocked unconscious when a frozen squid dropped from the sky and landed on his head. (1997)

9. In a remote region of Russia, hundreds of antique gold coins rained down on inhabitants; it was believed to have been treasure swept up by a storm. (1940)

10. After a rainstorm, dozens of golf balls poured down onto the streets of a Florida town; a waterspout was thought to be the cause. (1969)

was renting her house, and while Ann felt the rock should be hers to keep (she was the one with the bruise, after all!), her landlady disagreed. Years of legal battles followed, by the end of which there was little profit left to be gained. In the end, the Hodges meteorite was donated to the Alabama Museum of Natural History, where it remains to this day.

Not the happiest ending for Ann Hodges, alas—but what can you expect from a story that starts with a rude nap-time wake-up by a drop-in from outer space? Still, it's a good reminder of how much is going on way up there.

Space is, you might say, rocking it! ☺

Our advice? Keep an eye on the sky. After all, you never know when you're at the start of a day that's gonna go down in history.

HELLOOOO! ANYONE ELSE OUT THERE?

If there is one thing that many people would give just about anything to know, it is this: Is there intelligent life outside our solar system? We've read the books and seen the movies: aliens, **extraterrestrial** beings, smart space invaders coming in peace (or in war). Still, science fiction aside, it's hard not to wonder: What if there *are* living, breathing, thinking creatures on a planet other than Earth?

SETI (Search for Extraterrestrial Intelligence) is a group term used for people and organizations who are devoted to trying to answer that very question.

Beginning in 1960 with Frank Drake and his 26-meter radio telescope, SETI now spans countries all over the world, with scores of scientists and **laypeople** united in one goal: to seek out life in worlds beyond our own.

But what does that actually mean? Usually, the task involves large radio telescopes pointed up and out, scanning the friendly skies. What comes back is a torrent of space noise, which is converted into numbers. And what are they on the lookout for, these sharp-eyed cosmic detectives? Patterns. Repeating numbers or other signals that appear to be made on purpose. Things that look like someone trying to say (in their own

extraterrestrial: Not from Earth

laypeople: In this case, nonscientists

The Arecibo radio telescope as seen from the observation deck

alien language), "Hello! Anyone else out there?"

Soon after SETI was launched, there was reason to be hopeful. In 1977, a volunteer named Jerry Ehman noted a signal so strong that it seemed to surely be more than random space noise. He famously scribbled "Wow!" on his printout page, leading to this long-unexplained recording being called the "Wow! signal." For decades, however, nothing like that signal was ever repeated, and early enthusiasm for the possibility of an alien transmission gradually waned. As Ehman himself told the *Cleveland Plain Dealer* in 1994: "If it were intelligent beings sending a signal, they'd do it far more than once."

So you will understand the wild excitement of alien enthusiasts everywhere when in May 2017 . . . the message was very closely

echoed in a transmission picked up by the Arecibo telescope in Puerto Rico, which was pointed at a **red dwarf star** just 11 light-years from Earth called Ross 128. The University of Puerto Rico's Planetary Habitability Laboratory director, Abel Mendez, called the strange signals "broadband quasi-periodic nonpolarized pulses with very strong dispersion-like features." Which you'd better believe is way too scientific for us. Bottom line: It's purposeful. It's big. It's *real*.

red dwarf star: A relatively small and low-light star

But is it from aliens? According to International Space Research Coordinator Marsha Sales, "There is no way that this signal had an accidental origin. It's far too precise." And even more telling: Six months later, in November 2017, the signal was repeated. This time, *in perfect detail*. All of which means: it must have been sent intentionally.

Wow!

There's that amazing signal!

But by what . . . or whom?

Ross 128 is a star, which means it could have planets circling it.

A satellite dish
listens and waits

Several months after the transmission signal, scientists discovered
that one of those **exoplanets** (which they named Ross 128 b) is
theoretically capable of sustaining life. Similar in size to Earth,
this planet has a **habitable** atmosphere and early tests show that
part of its atmosphere is water
vapor—which means there may
be liquid water on the surface!

   Let's review the facts
about this star so far: (1) a
nonrandom transmission

exoplanets: Planets orbiting
a star that's not in our solar
system

habitable: Able to be lived on,
or to support life

that was (2) repeated precisely from (3) a nearby habitable planet.
Scientists are famously cautious creatures, so they are not yet
willing to come out and say "there are aliens talking to us from
outer space"—not until they see clear and measurable proof of said
aliens.

But the evidence so far is pretty compelling, don't you think?

Try It: Build Your Ideal Planet

Outer space is one of those mysteries that is endlessly fascinating and full of possibility. So let's put our "what if" hats on for a minute. What if you were to design your ideal planet? What would it need? How might it be structured?

Think about what a planet requires to support life, and go from there. Some things to write about:

* How long are the days? Nights? Seasons? Years?

* Does the planet have one sun or more? If more, how does this affect the planet's weather and other aspects?

* Is gravity the same as Earth's, or heavier, or lighter? What impact would this have on plant and animal life?

* What is the terrain like? What is the ocean/groundwater situation? Is there animal wildlife on this planet, and how might those creatures adapt based on the environmental conditions?

* Don't forget to give your planet a name.

Finally: Write a story set on your fictional planet!

SO THERE YOU HAVE IT! *A breakthrough in teleportation, an actual stone from space clocking some poor woman on the hip, and an outer-space transmission giving a strong indication of intelligent life on another planet. Which are true? Which is false? We know you know what to do. . . .*

PART 3

SCIENCE IN ACTION

Science can be wondrous, surprising, even mind-blowing.
Indeed, we found so many fascinating stories during the course
of our research that it was almost impossible for us to choose
which ones to include. But choose we did. Here, without further
ado, are some of our favorite science-related stories of all. But
don't just trust us, read them for yourself! (Seriously: don't trust
us. After all, some of these stories are outright lies.)

A.  You Can Call Me "Agent Spywing"

Sometimes, the world is a dark place. While we hope that you, our beloved readers, will always be in a place of safety, peace, and joy, there are times when things do go bad, when evil people touch a corner of our world in terrible ways. Some of the worst of these are terrorists, who tragically and violently

ARMÉE DE L'AIR

Looking good in a snazzy hood

A French army falconer works with a D'Artagnan Royal Eagle

attack innocent people for their own political ends. Thankfully, there are many people and organizations working to protect us—including soldiers, diplomats, and other government forces.

But what if there were *other* helpers to safeguard our lives and freedoms as well? What if there were creatures looking out for us by looking *down* on us from way up high?

It's time to meet some of the newest members of the war on terror: the French eagle squad. (If that wasn't clear enough, they are *literal* eagles!)

The cutting-edge program began on the southwestern French air force base of Mont-de-Marsan, when four golden eagles were hatched. Their nest? A drone. Yup, you read that right. The chicks were born right atop a deadly drone fighter.

Drones are very small, **unmanned** crafts, about the size of a model airplane. Commercial drones can be used by ordinary

Gotcha!

people for things like taking photos and videos from up in the air. Drones are also used by the military for defense and other types of operations.

But drones can also be turned to evil: they can be used by terrorists to attack peaceful populations. And *that* is why the eagle squad was raised—and what they are being trained to combat.

The first four hatchlings, named for Alexandre Dumas's famous **Musketeers**—Athos, Porthos, Aramis, and D'Artagnan—were raised to view the drones as prey. The young birds chased drones across the ground, being rewarded with meat

unmanned: With no pilot inside

Musketeers: *The Three Musketeers*, by Alexandre Dumas, is a classic novel—check it out!

Kevlar: Super-strong material that's nearly indestructible

when they made a catch. As the eagles grew and took flight, they were trained to hunt drones in the air.

Spot. Target. Attack!

The result? According to French air force general Jean-Christophe Zimmerman, these winged defenders are now able to spot drones from thousands of yards away and take them out swiftly and efficiently.

The project is still in development, but early results are very promising, and much more is on the way. Protective armor of leather and **Kevlar** is being designed for the Musketeers, along with a new base high in the Pyrenees Mountains. From this launching point they will be able to patrol French airspace, darting out with lightning speed to keep

Animals Did THAT?

It may sound unbelievable, but each of the animals below did the amazing tasks ascribed to them . . . all but one, that is. Can you sniff out the fake fact?

1. Airplane manufacturer Boeing once trained ferrets to string wires through interior passageways of aircraft too small for human technicians to reach.

2. A gorilla named Koko was taught sign language and could both understand and communicate using nearly 1,000 signs.

3. In the mid-1960s, the CIA implanted tiny transmitters into cats as part of their program to train feline superspies.

4. When her owner had a heart attack, a potbelly pig named Lulu broke through a gate and lay down in traffic until someone followed her home to save her owner's life.

5. In 2005, butterflies were taught to paint using a nontoxic paint mixture of sweet, colored liquid, resulting in surprisingly gorgeous art pieces that were sold to raise money for a butterfly conservation organization.

(Continued on next page)

those friendly skies clear and safe. A new brood of eagles is reportedly being groomed for action as well.

The technique of training eagles for defense has also been pursued in the Netherlands; who knows what country will be next? Maybe, one day soon, you will look up in the sky and spot a winged predator high over your home—wheeling, scoping, scanning for prey: not field mice and smaller birds, but for any signs of danger. Ready and waiting for the slightest provocation; ready to do their duty, from the high lofty sky to our home territory below.

Animals Did THAT? (continued)

6. In 2007, farmer Peter Houguez began feeding his cows carrots. He was surprised to find their milk turned pink.

7. A World War I dog named Stubby served on the front lines of 17 battles, finding wounded soldiers, warning of gas strikes, and more—finally being promoted to sergeant.

8. When Robert Biggs was attacked by a mountain lion while hiking, a nearby bear reportedly came to his defense and fought off the attacker.

9. Wendy Humphreys's cat kept jumping insistently on her breast; testing showed she had a cancerous tumor, which she was then able to get treated.

10. Starting in the 1960s, the US Navy began training dolphins to use their sonar to locate mines in the deep ocean.

LATER, GATOR!

Science can be a lot of things: It can be fun. It can be interesting. Sometimes it can be really complicated. But when it comes down to it, a lot of science is trying to understand how the world works—and then putting that knowledge to use in your own life. Sometimes when you do that, science can be downright miraculous!

Which is exactly what happened to the heroine of our next story.

On May 6, 2017, ten-year-old Juliana Ossa was enjoying a relaxing Saturday with her family at a lakeside park in Orlando, Florida. Sun! Splashing!

. . . Sneak attack?

That's right. With no warning at all, this casual

Excuse me, you have a crab in your teeth

outing took a turn from pleasantly ordinary to truly terrifying. As Juliana sat in the two-foot-deep water at the lake's edge, there was a sudden movement near her. A lurch followed, and a splash. Before Juliana could react, an alligator *grabbed her by the leg* in its powerful jaws!

Now, what's the first thing you would do in a situation like this? If you say "try to get away," then we are on the same page. But here's the thing: an alligator has one of the strongest bites on record—with several times more jaw force than even a lion or tiger! Juliana Ossa was four feet, seven inches tall. The gator was nearly nine feet long: so, almost twice her size, and *far* more than twice her strength.

There was no way this girl could just pry her foot back out of that gator's mouth. Once a gator has hold of its prey, it does *not* let it go willingly. Guess what else? A gator's next move, after grabbing something in its jaws, is often to dive deep and swim away. And a gator in water can move fast—up to 20 miles per hour.

Bottom line: Juliana needed to get her leg out of that gator's mouth, and *quick*, but it would not be easy.

In a panic, Juliana punched the gator on the forehead. It did not let go. Others quickly rushed to help, but no one knew how to get the gator to release Juliana before it took off with her.

Then Juliana remembered something. She had recently learned about alligator safety (this was Florida, after all!), and one of those defense tactics suddenly came to her mind. Moving quickly, Juliana

Warning: Do not try this at home!

shoved her fingers up the alligator's nostrils— all the way until she blocked the creature's airflow. What happened next? "It couldn't breathe," Juliana later told *Inside Edition*. "So it had to breathe through its mouth and open its mouth, and it let my leg out."

After that, things resolved quickly. Alligators tend to give up when their prey fights back, and this beast must have known it was outwitted. After the gator let go of Juliana's leg, she was transported to a nearby hospital. She received stitches in her leg and, thankfully, recovered well.

So there's a happy ending to this dire tale—and all because this girl not only paid attention to the way things around her work, but was smart and spirited enough to put that knowledge into action when she needed it most.

Try It: Ready for Something New?

It's a fact: The more you know, the more you can do. And you might just be surprised at the wide range of things you can learn about. Like Juliana learning how to subdue a rampaging alligator, is there a rare skill to be learned somewhere near you? Here are some tips to help you find out.

First, think about subjects that interest you, and any nearby places that touch on them:

* Museums: Art! Natural history! Science!

* Studios and craftsmanship operations: Pottery! Glassblowing! Woodworking!

* Family-run businesses and shops: Fishmongers! Butchers! Cheesemakers!

* And also: Farmers' markets! Craft fairs! Flea markets! Nature and wildlife preserves!

Don't forget to check your library or community bulletin boards or online postings for advertisements and notices and opportunities.

Now see what options are available for your age group and budget. Many organizations offer paid classes, but there are also free opportunities to be found: open houses, studio tours, information sessions, and more. Or just drop by and ask some questions!

Did you like what you learned? Dig deeper! Put your terrific Two Truths and a Lie research skills to good use and find out *more* about your new favorite subject.

TESLA'S "DEATH RAY" DISASTER

Have you heard the name Nikola Tesla? He was a brilliant scientist, inventor, and onetime employee of Thomas Edison who lived and worked in America in the late 1800s and early 1900s. Though best known for his contributions to our understanding of electricity and modern electrical systems, Tesla also dreamed up plans for new motors, radios, lights, and many other electronic devices. You probably use things built from his ideas every day. Without his work, our world would look very different than it does now.

Nikola Tesla

Wardenclyffe Tower in Long Island, New York

TESLA'S TOWER

Amazing Scheme of the Great Inventor to Draw Millions of Volts of Electricity Through the Air From Niagara Falls, and Then Feed It Out to Cities, Factories and Private Houses from the Tops of the Towers WITHOUT WIRES.

Yes, certainly made his But, unfortunately, his marks weren't all good ones. Just ask Siberia.

As Tesla's understanding of electricity grew, he became convinced that it was possible to transmit electrical current without using any cords or wires. And he spent a great deal of his time and money trying to figure out exactly how to do it. In 1901, he started construction on a new lab on Long Island, New York, so he could test his theories. He also built a powerful transmitter capable of beaming out electricity, which he named Wardenclyffe Tower. By 1908, however, he'd shown little success and his investors were getting nervous. He had to do something impressive.

At the same time, the explorer Admiral Robert Peary's attempt to reach the North Pole was making headlines around the world. Before the expedition left, Tesla told Peary that he would contact him during the journey. "Be on the lookout for signals in the sky,"

he said. Tesla's plan was to send a bolt of energy from New York toward Peary's camp hundreds of miles north and, at the very least, create an unforgettable light show.

On June 30, 1908, at around seven p.m., Tesla aimed the transmitter in what he thought was the direction of Peary's camp on Ellesmere Island in the northernmost reaches of Canada. He flipped the switch. Oh, did he put on a show! Unfortunately, the show wasn't at all what—or where—he had expected it to be.

On the other side of the world, residents near Siberia's Lake Baikal in northern Russia were just starting their day when a bright-blue streak shot across the sky. Next came an intense flash of light and a thunderous boom. People were knocked off their feet and windows shattered for miles around. It felt like an earthquake, or like an enormous bomb had gone off. Many trees in the region—more than forty million—were knocked down flat, all pointing in the same direction.

Trees flattened by the death ray near Tunguska

What's in a Name?

We love lists! We also love inventors. Sometimes, if an invention—or its inventor—is lucky enough, the object takes on the name of its creator. Here is a list of amazing everyday items that are actually named after the person who invented them. All but one, that is . . .

1. SANDWICH: Earl of Sandwich, 1700s
2. FERRIS WHEEL: George Washington Ferris, 1893
3. SAXOPHONE: Adolphe Sax, 1840s
4. BALLET: Clothilde de Ballet, 1722
5. JACUZZI: the Jacuzzi brothers, 1968
6. GRAHAM CRACKER: Reverend Sylvester Graham, early 1800s
7. LOGANBERRY: Judge J. H. Logan, 1883
8. MORSE CODE: Samuel Morse, 1830s–40s
9. RUBIK'S CUBE: Erno Rubik, 1974
10. TUPPERWARE: Earl Silas Tupper, 1946

Tesla was lucky. As far as we know, no one was killed by his "death ray," as it came to be called. His energy beam had hit a sparsely populated area. If it had hit a city instead, millions of people could have died—and Tesla would be famous for having caused an epic disaster, instead of his many useful inventions.

Fortunately, Tesla learned his lesson. He ceased all experiments on wireless electricity, closed his lab, and sold Wardenclyffe Tower, which was soon dismantled by its new owner. It was an unfortunate end to an amazing career, to be sure . . . but it could have been much, much worse.

WHOA! WE NEED A MOMENT *to catch our breath after all that excitement. Let's recap: we've got a fleet of drone-disabling eagles; a ten-year-old girl who took out an alligator; and an accidental death ray invented in 1908. They can't all be true—and they aren't. But which is which? Have at it, researchers!*

A. DEATH COMES FROM THE DEEP

There are some dates that loom so large in history that they cannot be forgotten. One of these days was November 22, 1963—the day that John F. Kennedy, the 35th president of the United States, was killed in Dallas, Texas. Clear across the country, however, this date also looms large for reasons that are completely different, but also dark and deadly.

Our story begins on the Staten Island Ferry, which shuttles passengers between Staten Island and Manhattan, in New York City. The free ferry service has been in operation since 1817, running 24 hours a day, 7 days a week, 365 days a year, with boats leaving every 20 to 30 minutes. It's usually a safe, comfortable, uneventful ride.

But not *this* one.

Just before four o'clock on this cold November predawn morning, the water was choppy. Unusually choppy, eyewitnesses would say later—but at the time, nothing seemed too out of the ordinary. A ferryboat called the *Cornelius G. Kolff* departed Saint George Terminal, making good time toward Whitehall Terminal in Manhattan.

About halfway to its destination, though, things began to get strange. The water started doing some serious **churning**. "It looked

The Staten Island Ferry and Statue of Liberty

like a storm was coming, but there was no storm," Paula Awer, an eyewitness, later told *Time* magazine.

churning: Swirling and moving vigorously in place

It was a short ride to the final destination, so the boat pushed on. But it would never make it to the dock. Less than a mile from shore, for no evident reason, the ferry suddenly sank below the waves—resulting, tragically, in the loss of all 408 passengers aboard.

But the strangest part of this story was yet to come: One of only two bystanders to witness the tragedy from shore, Awer described what she saw as not a seafaring weather disaster or some

Pieces from the wreckage

type of mechanical failure, but something much more sinister. "It looked like the boat was being sucked or pulled under," she said. "It was there . . . and then it just wasn't."

What could have been to blame? Awer and others speculated: Could some kind of sea creature have dragged a 500-ton boat underwater in mere minutes, without time for the crew to even radio for help? And there was more strange evidence to come. When several outer panels of the ferry were recovered after the disaster, they showed clear signs of enormous suction marks.

According to local historian Joseph Reginella, there is only one possible culprit for this type of deadly stealth: a giant squid. These elusive creatures are found the world over, but are notoriously timid, and tend to keep to the deep ocean. They have, however, been known to venture up nearer the surface for food.

According to *National Geographic*, the largest recorded giant

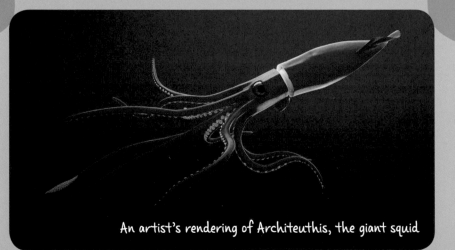

An artist's rendering of Architeuthis, the giant squid

squid to date measured 59 feet long—almost a third the length of the 207-foot ferry—but researchers believe that, if it was indeed a creature of this type that attacked the *Kolff*, this specimen must have been even larger.

With little evidence available, much at this point remains subject to speculation. Many scientists feel that a giant squid attack in New York harbor is unlikely; some have even suggested a corporate cover-up to mask **negligence** or other causes of the disaster. But Reginella wants the facts out there so people can make up their own minds. To that end, he established the Staten Island Ferry Disaster Memorial Museum, complete with a cast-bronze monument in Battery Park to honor the victims.

Meanwhile, clear across the

Speaking of Statues . . .

Plaques, memorials, and statues are an important way to remember people and events of the past. There are countless magnificent ones in the world; but there are lots of others that are just plain weird. Check out these ten jaw-dropping statues that actually exist—except, of course, for the one that doesn't.

1. A statue of Lieutenant-Governor Charles Latrobe that is literally upside down, with Latrobe's head on the ground and the pedestal rising into the air above him (Melbourne, Australia)

2. A giant hand, 36 feet tall and half buried in the sand, with just an enormous thumb and fingers pointing skyward (Atacama, Chile)

3. A sculpture of a crocodile crawling out of a manhole and eating a man whose head is shaped like a bag of money (Brooklyn, New York)

4. A full-color sculpture of Superman face-planting on the street, a temporary installment tied to the Jewish Museum (Berlin, Germany)

(Continued on next page)

Speaking of Statues . . . (continued)

5. A monument showing a mouse wearing glasses and knitting a DNA strand, to commemorate the creatures who were sacrificed in the name of science (Novosibirsk, Russia)

6. Funded by Kickstarter, a statue of Nikola Tesla holding a lightbulb—set up to provide free Wi-Fi to all passersby (Silicon Valley, California)

7. A huge sculpture of an apple with a worm crawling down the side—the piece is so big that a person can crawl into the hole and come out the other side (Johannesburg, South Africa)

8. An enormous sculpture of the head and shoulders of Confucius rising out of a pool of water; the lifelike chest moves slowly up and down as though breathing (Shanghai, China)

9. A statue created in 1546 of a creepy bogeyman holding a bag of babies—and eating one! (Bern, Switzerland)

10. A 25-foot sculpture of a shark, called Headington Shark, crashing headfirst into the roof of an ordinary house; designed to commemorate the atomic bombing of Nagasaki (Oxfordshire, England)

negligence: When things aren't done properly, with bad results

Statue dedicated to the passengers and crew

country and not many hours later, President Kennedy's tragic death shook the nation to its core. In the resulting chaos, the Staten Island Ferry Disaster sank from view. But Reginella, and others like him, have sworn they will not rest until the mystery is solved once and for all.

"The truth is out there," Awer insists. "Sooner or later, someone is bound to find the scientific proof."

B. YOUR DINNER IS IN THE PRINTER, DEAR!

Okay, so, there are printers—and then, there are *3D* printers.

You may have heard of these, you may have even seen one in action, but if not, here's a primer. The roots of 3D printing date back to the early 1980s (and doesn't most of the really cool stuff, hmmm? ☺) and the work of Hideo Kodama and later Charles Hull.

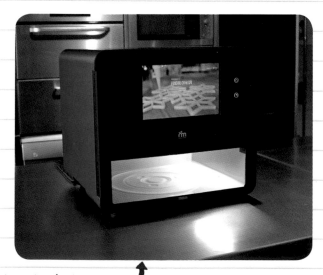

Meet Foodini!

Over the next three decades, the process would be refined, eventually to produce the 3D printers we have today.

How do they work? First, a complex printing machine is

stocked with a material such as plastic, metal, or graphite. The printer is connected to a computer that is programmed with a specific design. Press a few buttons and the machine goes to work, setting out the material one layer at a time until . . . presto! The finished object pops out of the printer ready to be put to use.

Today, almost anything can be cranked out of a 3D printer. Replacement parts for decades-old machines; **prosthetic limbs** made to fit the person wearing them; a perfect replica of Iron Man's suit, custom-tailored to size. There is even a growing movement that is working with cells and tissue—though the technology has not been perfected, they one day hope to be able to print internal organs for human transplants! (Whoa.)

A Foodini in action

All that work designing 3D printer models could sure make a person hungry, don't you think?

Wait a minute . . . That gives us an idea.

And someone else had the *exact same one.*

Young ladies and gentlemen, allow me to introduce you to the Foodini. Created by the Barcelona-based start-up Natural Machines, this revolutionary 3D printer does not use plastic or other standard filaments to do its creating—instead, it uses edible, fresh ingredients to print up a full meal. For example: Pop in some dough ingredients and a cheese filling, press a button, and you've got . . . ravioli! In 2015 the Foodini was named by CNN

prosthetic limbs: Artificial replacement body parts

BeeHex is bringing 3D printing to food, one pizza at a time

One Foodini, two Foodini . . .

as one of their "tech superheroes" to watch. Company cofounder Lynette Kucsma envisions a day when food-printing robots are as ordinary and commonplace as microwave ovens are today.

There's another area in which 3D food printing is getting a lot of attention: space food. Up until now, space food has been famously unappetizing. Weight and volume have to come first, which means astronauts have to turn in their gourmet foodie cards at the boarding dock. But in recent years **NASA** has been funding research on this topic, and the field has seen some new and exciting developments. In a 2015 "Print Your Own Space Food" challenge, a group from Macedonia known as Team Kokino took first place with their working prototype of a 3D printer: options included food, drink, and dessert, all available at the press of a button. Around the same time, California-based start-up BeeHex created a robot called Chef 3D that can print out a pizza in any shape you like.

Taking it back to Earth, there's even a London-based restaurant called Food Ink whose claim to fame is that *every single thing in the restaurant*— from tables and chairs to silverware to the food on

NASA: National Aeronautics and Space Administration, the government agency in charge of monitoring and exploring outer space

Your freshly printed meal awaits!

your plate—was created using a 3D printer. Now that's a feat!

While some consumers are uncomfortable with the idea of bringing technology into yet another part of our everyday lives, fans of 3D food printing rave about its health potential: after all, users can input all their own real ingredients, which means you know exactly what you are eating, with no added chemicals or preservatives.

One thing's for sure—3D printing is here to stay. And, whether on Earth or in space, it seems that the applications (and, some say, the advantages) are infinite.

Talk It Out: What Would YOU Print?

What is futuristic thinking today could soon be our everyday reality, so there's no time like the present to ponder the possibilities. If you could print up anything you wanted, anytime, what would it be? Why? What materials would be needed? What would you use it for? Would anyone else want that item? How would you market your product? What might the downsides be?

Get ready, because the future is almost here!

THAT'S WHAT WE CALL A ONE-MAN OPERATION

//

Sometimes you look at people who do incredible things and you think, "I could *never* do that!" (Spoiler alert: you'll be saying this soon; we guarantee it.) But the truth is, sometimes you don't have a choice.

Which brings us to the story of Dr. Leonid Rogozov. Born in Eastern Siberia, Russia, this young **surgeon** joined up with a team of scientists in 1960 and set off for Antarctica as part of the sixth Soviet Antarctic expedition. Rogozov was the only doctor on the trip.

At first, all went as planned. But on the morning of April 29, 1961, there was a hint of the trouble ahead. Rogozov hadn't been feeling well: he was weak, nauseated, and running a slight fever.

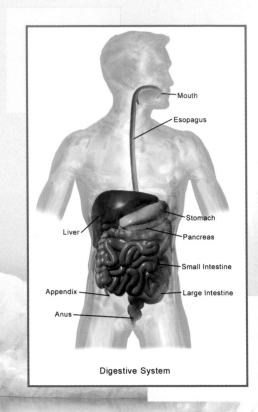

Digestive System

Labels: Mouth, Esopagus, Stomach, Liver, Pancreas, Small Intestine, Appendix, Large Intestine, Anus

Even more concerning, though, was a growing pain in his lower right **abdomen**. As a doctor, Rogozov recognized these symptoms for what they were: acute appendicitis.

What does this mean to us nondoctors? The appendix is a tiny little pouch inside your lower belly. Most of the time it just hangs out in there, looking cool, not doing much of anything. But when things go wrong in appendix land, they *really* go wrong. Appendicitis, an infection of the appendix, is rare, but it can be dangerous. Pain goes from sharp to sharper. The infected appendix swells. If it's not treated, the appendix can eventually burst, spreading deadly toxins throughout your whole body. (At that point, it's very often game over.)

There is only one remedy: take out that appendix, before it takes out *you.*

So now we go back to the sixth Soviet Antarctic research team—a team that was, don't forget, way down in the Antarctic, thousands of miles from anyone or anything else. Even worse, severe weather had cut off any chance of transport back to civilization. And the only doctor on the team was the one with appendicitis.

So who was going to operate on Dr. Leonid Rogozov to save his life?

The good doctor knew there was only one answer to this question. In his diary he wrote: "This is it . . . I have to think through the only possible way out: to operate on myself. . . . It's almost impossible . . . but I can't just fold my arms and give up."

surgeon: A doctor who cuts open a patient's body to remove or fix internal problems

abdomen: Stomach area

There was, after all, no one else.

And so Rogozov went to work. He prepared himself for surgery. He set up a mirror facing his belly so he could see what he was doing. A mechanic and a meteorologist from the base acted as his surgical assistants—passing him instruments and shifting the mirror so he could see better. In about a two-hour operation, he performed an astonishing self-appendectomy, locating his own inflamed appendix and cutting it clean out of his body.

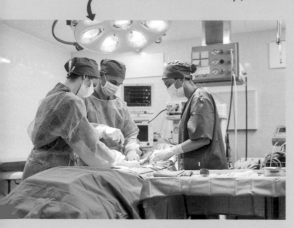

This is what it's *supposed* to look like

Miraculously, the operation was a success. Within five days, Rogozov's temperature was back to normal, and a few days later he removed his own stitches. Two weeks after his operation, he was back to work.

Rogozov continued his efforts with the team in Antarctica for another year until his return home. But his inspiring feat did not go unrecognized: the government gave him a prestigious award for his bravery. More important, his story endures as an essential reminder that you really don't know what you can do until you have to—and until you decide to *try*.

Try It: Mirror, Mirror

We certainly do NOT advise any surgical experimentation, but mirrors can be fun to experiment with. Gather up some small mirrors and try these activities yourself:

* Hold one mirror facing away from you while looking into another mirror. How many reflections do you see?

* Aim a flashlight or laser pointer toward a mirror at an angle and try to predict where the beam will appear on the wall.

* Set a blank sheet of paper below a mirror. While looking only at the paper's reflection in the mirror, try to draw a picture on the paper. With another blank sheet, try to write your name so you can read it correctly in the mirror. Move the mirror to a different angle or position and try again to see how that changes the experience.

* Set up a double mirror by placing two mirrors edge to edge like an open book. Place an object near where the mirrors meet. How many objects do you see? Change the angle of the mirrors and observe how that changes the reflections.

* Place a blank sheet of paper below the double mirror. Draw a line connecting the two mirrors and observe the reflection. Again, change the angle of the mirrors and see what shapes you can observe in the reflection.

* Now, imagine aiming a flashlight or laser pointer at one of the sides of the double mirror. Try to predict where the beam would appear on the wall. Test your theory.

STORIES UPON STORIES UPON STORIES! *In this chapter we've heard a harrowing tale of destruction from the deep, learned about incredible advances in 3D printing, and gasped at a man who cut out his own appendix. They are all unbelievable, but they can't all be true. You know what to do. And . . . go!*

A. IF YOU DREAM IT, YOU CAN . . . SEE IT?!

What's the coolest dream you've ever had? This author used to regularly have dreams that were like actual movies: complete with title, credits, and all. Upon waking, there was always that momentary rush of trying to write down the movie title so as to look it up later and see if it was a real movie. (It never was.) This remains a high point of said author's dream life.

But we digress.

The sleeping brain has always been a big-time mystery, and one thing the brain is best at is keeping secrets about how it works. But in recent years, scientists have begun to crack some of those secrets—with some pretty exciting results.

In 2005, University of Kyoto professor Yukiyasu Kamitani published a paper on his research into decoding images from brain activity, in the journal *Nature Neuroscience*. By using **fMRI** imaging, Kamitani and his team were able to record and show rough patterns in test subjects' brain activity.

Now, fast-forward nearly a decade; that's when things *really* started hopping.

In a groundbreaking 2013 study, Kamitani's team selected three participants, who went to sleep for

fMRI: Functional magnetic resonance imaging; a machine that measures brain activity by recording blood flow

blocks of time over a ten-day period while inside an fMRI scanner *and* while connected to an **EEG**. This study had a twist, though: the machines were hooked up to the team's special predictive computer model—a "dream-reading machine."

EEG: Electroencephalogram machine; a machine that records the brain's electrical activity

algorithm: A set of rules to be followed for problem solving, often by computers

But what *was* that "dream-reading machine"? Ah, there's the corker! This excellent and highly technical program was shaped as follows: first, subjects are shown images while awake. Let's say: a car. The program records the patterns of brain activity. With time and data, the **algorithm** in the program is able to recognize various objects as they are shown—using *only* the scans from the subjects' brains. ("Look!" the technician might say, studying the computer data. "Now they're showing an image of a car.")

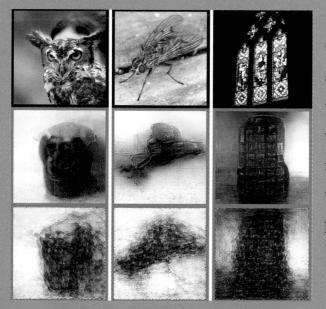

Next, the subjects sleep. Once they begin to dream, the scientists wake the subject up and ask them what they were just seeing. Again, the machine continues to record their brain activity. Gradually, patterns emerge that can

Kamitani's team also has computers "read people's minds" (bottom two rows) to predict what they were looking at while awake (top)

tie specific brain activity connected to seeing certain images—such as the car above—whether in real life *or* in dreams. (Bear in mind that we are making up this specific example, but that is generally how the study operated.)

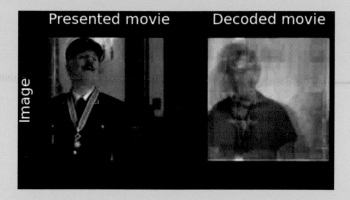

Computers at the Gallant Lab reconstruct what movie a person is watching

So after hundreds of tests on subjects both awake and dreaming, the predictive model developed by the researchers over the course of this study was able to predict with 60% accuracy the broad topics experienced by the subjects in their dreams. In other words—it can tell (some of) what people are dreaming about—while they are still asleep!

In a similar vein is the work of Jack Gallant, a **neuroscientist** from University of California, Berkeley. In a 2011 study published in the journal *Current Biology*, Gallant describes software that can not only scan subjects' brains to recognize patterns, but then transfers that data onto a screen into a roughly viewable series of images—like a mini film window inside the brain! "We are opening a window into the

neuroscientist: Someone who studies the brain or nervous system

movies in our minds," says Gallant. Can you imagine if you could watch a movie of your own dream? Or someone else's?

Needless to say, all of this is in a pretty early stage of development. But with these breakthroughs, it's not hard to imagine a near future world where a dream is not just a movie you watch while you're asleep—but something you can also record, save, and share with your friends.

Whether that would be a good or a bad thing, though, is a whole other story. Would you want someone else to watch a movie of *your* dreams?

Try It: Keep a Dream Journal

Do you ever remember your dreams? However much or little of your memories remain upon waking tends to quickly disappear once you begin your day. To get to know your dreams a bit better, try this:

* Keep a special notebook right by your bed, with a pen or pencil handy.

* When you first wake up, before getting out of bed or talking to anyone, write down as much as you remember from what you were dreaming before you awoke.

* Be detailed! Make note of specific names, places, and other memorable elements.

* Do this for at least a week—or longer if you enjoy it. You may find that the more you practice noticing and remembering, the more there will be to recall.

Some people think that the subconscious mind can send us messages through our dreams; other people just have fun recording them. What do *you* think?

B. AND THEY SAY YELLING NEVER SOLVES ANYTHING

There's a lot of talk these days about **renewable energy** and how we can conserve the Earth's resources by using them in the most efficient way possible. Countries all around the world are joining this effort, making big investments into channeling Earth's renewable resources—such as sun, wind, and water—and turning them into energy to be used for heating, electricity, and more.

Not every nation has access to all these elements, however. Despite being a global leader in industry and technology, the island nation of Singapore is severely limited by its lack of natural resources. With more and more energy being needed to support its growing

population, many leading minds are at work on this pressing problem.

One new leader in the field is University of Singapore physicist Valerie Pan. Over the last 30 years, Pan has focused her research on analyzing the link between potential energy (stored up, like the energy in a battery) and kinetic energy (energy that is turned into motion or action).

The idea for her research was planted by a most unusual source: Singapore traffic. Stuck one day in a bumper-to-bumper slog, Pan started noticing the reactions of drivers in the lanes near her. "We hadn't moved in nearly an hour," she recalled in a *Scientific American* write-up. "People were furious, they were yelling!" But in a uniquely scientific twist, Pan started noticing how much energy these angry people were expelling.

renewable energy: Power from a source that doesn't decrease as it is used, or is replaced naturally

What if, she thought, that energy could be put to use?

Over a decade later, in April 2018, Pan released the beta version of her groundbreaking invention:

Valerie Pan, hard at work solving problems

the Yellerator. This complex device, about the size of a megaphone, is outfitted with sophisticated sensors that are not only able to register potential energy stored in sound waves, but are also able to store and convert it

to kinetic energy. What we're saying is that the more you shout into the Yellerator, the more power you get. Talk about useful!

So, what *can* that power be used for? Pan is the first to stress that this project is in its very early stages. She has hooked up the first Yellerator to a simple scooter, with modest results; the stored energy from test studies was able to power the machine for a full hour of driving. We're talking a no-gas-needed scooter ride for a full hour, powered only by the sound of your shouting.

As far as Pan is concerned, this is the start of something huge. "We've already doubled the output capacity from stored power," she told *Scientific American*. "Within five years, it will be tenfold."

And if anger can be turned into fuel, what other emotional

energy might there be to tap into? With seven billion human beings on this planet—each one complete with their own emotional spectrum of anger, fear, joy, and more—*that* sounds to us like a renewable natural resource well worth exploring: the sweet sound of successful enterprise.

Talk It Out:
Failure . . . or Opportunity?

"Most of science is well-documented failure." —Jason Haaheim

In other words, in order to do something incredible, amazing, brand-new—you often have to do things wrong first. Sometimes you have to do things wrong a *lot*. Take some time to discuss the quote above and the principle behind it. How can failing help you learn new things? Can you learn to fail *better*? Is there something you can do poorly now in order to gain new knowledge or improve your technique, so that you might be successful later on?

What would you most like to try if you knew you couldn't fail? How bad would failing at that thing really be? Could failure be, ultimately, success? Might it be worth a try, no matter what the outcome?

C. I, ROBOT. I, WORM.

What is the brain? There's an obvious answer to this: the pale tissue inside your skull that acts as your body's control center. But let's go a step deeper—because the brain isn't just the boss of your body, keeping all your systems operating in tip-top shape; it's also a scatter-mash of electrical signals, which translate into your mind and your thoughts. These signals and impulses make up your consciousness; the home, you might say, of your truest self.

Now, what if you could move someone's brain into another body? That would be incredibly risky, of course, but remember: a brain's thoughts are nothing more than electrical signals. So, what if you could duplicate just those electrical signals in another brain? Would that mean you could copy a person's

3D model of a worm's brain and nervous system

consciousness, the part that does the actual thinking?

Science is still a long way off from being able to accomplish that. Well—in humans, anyway. Outside of humanity is another story. Today we're going to shrink the subject down to a much smaller scale.

Meet my wee worm pal, *Caenorhabditis elegans*—known as

Wiggle on, tiny friends!

C. elegans among friends. It's tiny, just about one millimeter long (that's 0.03—or 3/100—of an inch). *C. elegans* is a great favorite among **researchers**; it's small, easy to raise, and it's one of the simplest organisms that has its own nervous system. It's also **translucent**, which makes its internal organs easy to study.

In 2014, a group of researchers known as OpenWorm undertook an amazing feat: to conduct the first consciousness transfer of a living creature. And what better candidate than the well-studied and thoroughly documented *C. elegans*?

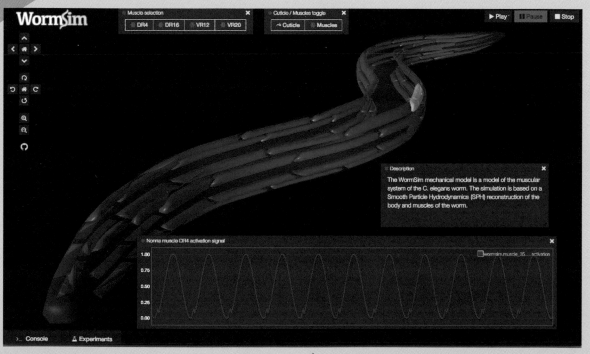

A mechanical model of worm muscles

Weird and Wacky Science!

What WILL scientists think of next? We have no idea! The fact is, they've come up with some pretty mind-blowing things already. If you're not sure about that, check out these ten hard-to-believe scientific studies or experiments. And they're all TRUE!
All but one, that is . . .

1. Behavioral psychologists from Albany Medical College ran experiments to test whether rats preferred hearing music by Beethoven, music by Miles Davis, or silence. (Silence came first, then Beethoven. Sorry, Miles!)

2. University of Lincoln's Dr. Anna Wilkinson did a study in social recognition by training a red-footed tortoise to yawn on command. (The yawn was not contagious to fellow tortoises.)

3. Neurology professor Peter Snyder of Brown University ran a study that showed that when people need to pee really badly, they have a difficult time problem-solving or making decisions. (Who'd have thought it?)

4. Researchers from the University of Cape Town ran a study to determine whether brownies are better eaten with or without ice cream. (Results were split almost exactly in half.)

(Continued on next page)

Over years of diligent work, all 302 **neurons** within *C. elegans* were mapped. This information was fed into a computer program developed by OpenWorm—step-by-step, first figuring out what each connection did and then recording that information in the software.

So, now you have this worm-consciousness, and it's all stored inside your computer. What next? Scientists did the obvious thing: they built a robot out of Legos, of course. (This is a satisfying solution to many problems, by the way.) Once this simple robot was ready, scientists copied every one of those electrical signals they had reproduced from *C. elegans*—and transferred

5. *Psychological Science* published the results of an experiment showing that when subjects lean to the left, doing so makes the Eiffel Tower (and presumably other structures?) look smaller.

6. *Polar Biology* published a study calculating the pressure and trajectory of the projectile poop of penguins. (For the curious: it travels an average of 16 inches.)

7. University of Minnesota researchers filled a pool with syrup in order to see if there was a difference between swimming in water and swimming in syrup. (No difference!)

8. A professor from Keio University ran years-long studies to show that pigeons could tell the difference between "good" and "bad" art, and the difference between certain famous artists.

9. Duke University scientists ran a study to determine why the bearcat smells like buttered popcorn. (That is the actual scent of their pee!)

10. University of California researcher Robert Cornish developed a "resurrection machine," which he used to bring two dead puppies back to life.

all that information over to the robot.

We can imagine that at this point, there was a bit of breath-holding.

Would the transfer work? What would the robot do? After all, the scientists had not programmed in any instructions. They had not told the software to do or act in any particular way. They just copied those neuron signals from the creature's brain.

Amazingly, after the transfer

researchers: People who study something particular in science

translucent: Partially see-through

neurons: Cells that transmit electrical impulses

The worm-robot in action

was complete, the robot acted exactly as the worm would have—
moving forward and back in response to touch, reacting to food,
etc. Basically, the robot seemed to "think" it was the worm.

So, *was* the robot truly a *C. elegans*? This is a whole other
question, which we are not going to debate today. But it's safe to

say that the implications here—for science, and for humanity—are plentiful and amazing.

Despite this thrilling development, there's little chance of a human consciousness being uploaded anytime soon. Remember those 302 neurons inside *C. elegans*? Remember how the scientists had to map and individually record each one? Well, the human brain has over *80 billion neurons*. So, yeah. There's still a ways to go.

But don't forget that somewhere in the world, there is a creature that is part worm, part robot—and all scientific breakthrough.

ALL GOOD THINGS MUST *come to an end, and that is nearly true for this book. But first, there is one more trifecta to triangulate. Can science really see inside a person's dreams? Is it possible to drive a scooter using stored-up sound energy? Was a worm's mind really put into a Lego body? Two are a yes and one is a no, people. Time to get busy!*

RESEARCH GUIDE

Every time you go online, you are faced with a barrage of information from a multitude of sources. The internet is great: it's the information superhighway, after all! You can type in a simple search and get over a million hits almost instantly. But, with virtually anyone anywhere having the ability to post anything they want, how can you know which results to trust and what to believe? Let's be honest, sometimes the internet feels more like the *mis*information superhighway.

And it's not just the internet, either. People make mistakes, even in books, newspapers, magazines, and on TV. Other times they're outright lying, whether to trick you or just to be entertaining. One thing's for sure: you can't trust everything you read, see, or hear.

Figuring out the truth can be a fun challenge sometimes, as we hope it has been in this book. But it can also be serious business: Following the wrong information can put relationships, reputations, money, health, and even lives at risk.

So, what's a reader to do?

First, check your common sense. Does it seem believable . . . or too outlandish to be true? This is a great starting point, but beware:

it often only goes so far. There are all kinds of unbelievable but true things about our world, and many very real things definitely defy common sense! And many things that seem like they could or should be true are actually not true at all. So, common sense is a great starting point, but it should never be your final stop.

Second, see if it fits with facts you already know are true. If a story contradicts something that is already well established, then its truthfulness should definitely be questioned.

Third, question what you *want* to be true. We humans are often blinded by our own hopes into believing things that we really wish were real. Psychologists call this "confirmation bias." But once you're aware that it exists, you'll (hopefully!) be less likely to fall for it.

Finally, always—ALWAYS—evaluate the sources of the information, if they're provided . . . and if they're not, try to find your own! How can you tell if a source is a good one? Here are a few characteristics to look for:

Currency: How timely is the information? When was it published? When was it updated? Is the timing appropriate for the topic?

Relevance: How closely does the information relate to the topic? Did the authors use the best sources available?

Authority: Who wrote and/or published the information? Are they qualified? Is there a way to contact them?

Accuracy: How correct is the content itself? Are there any obvious errors? Has it been reviewed? Does it match information found elsewhere?

Purpose: Why does the information exist? Was it written to inform, entertain, or persuade? Who paid for it, and what was their motivation?

As you can see, the best way to not get tricked is to remember to ask a lot of questions. And if you can't find the answers yourself, ask an expert to help you out.

Don't know any experts in that particular topic? Ask a librarian! Curating, organizing, and finding information is what they do best, and they'll be glad you asked.

PART 1: IT'S ELEMENTAL

CHAPTER 1: EARTH

The Sahara really was underwater millions of years ago, they really have found fossils of marine creatures there, and the Richat Structure is a very real phenomenon that can indeed be seen from space—and yet, the "A Whirl without a Pool" story is not true. The so-called Eye of Africa never had anything to do with an ancient ocean-sucking whirlpool. Instead, it is believed to be a geologic dome that was worn down over time by erosion.

Incredible Islands

San Serriffe is a fictional island described in a seven-page special report published on April 1, 1977, in *The Guardian*, a British newspaper. (Get it? April first? ☺)

CHAPTER 2: WATER

Arctic frost flowers are a real phenomenon, and they're really cool (literally!). The explanation given in "Ice-capades" for how they're made, however, is completely false. Frost flowers are actually formed when very cold, very dry air pulls moisture away from the surface of newly frozen ice. The air then quickly refreezes that moisture, which adds to the growing frost flower—no hail required!

Spectacular Lakes

There is no Spiral Lake shaped like a perfect spiral in Guatemala. Lake Manicouagan in Quebec, Canada, is shaped like a ring, though.

CHAPTER 3: AIR

For better or worse, windmills won't be chasing away Holland's rain clouds anytime soon. First, windmills don't actually blow anything—the wind blows them! Second, altering natural weather patterns is probably a bad idea for a lot of reasons, which Google most certainly knows. They do apparently have a good sense of humor, however, since they launched their own version of our "Windmills to the Rescue" story as an April Fool's Day prank back in 2017.

Impressive Volcanoes

Eyjafjallajökull did erupt in 2010 and its ash cloud forced many flight cancellations, leaving millions of air travelers stranded on both sides of the Atlantic. Fortunately, all potential crashes were avoided.

CHAPTER 4: UNCANNY CHEMISTRY

As much as we love the idea of a well brimming with healthy soda, "Quite a Sweet Story!" is a fake. There are many true elements, though. All those facts about clean drinking water, and the parts of the world—including in the United States—that need it, are real. And Oxfam is indeed doing amazing work with its program to teach local villagers around the world to build their own wells. Nigeria is also a leading exporter of papayas, and Yeshua is the real name of a papaya farm in the Ibadan region of the country. But, sadly, there are no natural soda springs there.

Our Weird Earth

As far as we know, there are no such things as glass beetles. Wouldn't it be cool if there were, though?

CHAPTER 5: FREAKY PHYSICS

On May 10, 2017, a website called *Focus Times* really did publish an article warning that fidget spinners could potentially affect Earth's gravity and orbit. Fortunately, it was all a hoax. There is zero scientific evidence for that article or for our own "Fidget Spinners' Revenge" story. So, spin all you want, or don't; gravity won't be affected either way. And if you get enough people together playing with their fidget spinners at the same time, be sure to call Guinness. You just might snag a world record after all!

Amazing After-Death Doings

Edgar Allan Poe did take his wife's death extremely hard, but he did not carry her remains around with him in any form, including in a snuffbox.

CHAPTER 6: SURPRISING SPACE

"Helloooo! Anyone Else Out There?" Not yet, alas. This story is the fake. Once again, there's a lot of real stuff layered in here. SETI is a real organization; the Wow! signal really happened; and Ross 128 is a real red dwarf star. The missing connections, though, are pure fiction. There was no precisely repeated signal. The transmission that appeared to issue from Ross 128 was identified as probably coming from Earth-orbiting satellites, bounced back by the distant star. And while Ross 128 b has been flagged as *likely* to have a habitable atmosphere, this is not yet a proven fact. At least as of the time this is going to print. . . . Stay tuned for future developments in space, y'all!

Take a Count of This!

There is no unit of measurement called the Sneeze Effect, although if you yourself suffer from seasonal allergies, you might feel there should be. (Achoo!)

What Else Is Falling from the Sky?

With everything that's falling from the sky already, you would think that a windfall of macarons wouldn't be too much to ask for. But alas, that listing is the fake, to your treat-loving authors' great regret!

CHAPTER 7: AMAZING

We'll admit this one was a bit tricky, because even our fake story had an extra dose of truth in it. Tesla really did devote much of his time and money to developing wireless electricity and there really was an event in Siberia in 1908 like the one in "Tesla's 'Death Ray' Disaster." Alas, the two had nothing to do with each other. It's believed that the trees were knocked down by the shock wave from a meteorite exploding just before it hit the ground. And neither Tesla nor any other scientist ever figured out how to build a globe-spanning "death ray." Thank goodness!

Animals Did THAT?

To our knowledge, no artist-butterflies do or have ever existed. It's fun to imagine those paintings, though, isn't it?

What's in a Name?

Clothilde de Ballet did not invent ballet. It's actually a French word that comes from the Italian word *balleto*, which comes from the late Latin word *ballare*, which means "to dance." (Like, at a ball, for example.)

CHAPTER 8: UNBELIEVABLE

The tragic death of President John F. Kennedy is all too real. The Staten Island Ferry Disaster, however, as chronicled in "Death Comes from the Deep," is a fake—a most elaborate fake, we might add, conceived by artist Joseph Reginella, who first told the story to his eleven-year-old nephew. The monument he later created was set up in various spots as a prank on passersby, though the city of New York did not approve and sent representatives to take it down within several days.

Speaking of Statues . . .

That giant apple statue, complete with crawlable wormhole, does sound pretty amazing. Alas, it's the fake! Unless someone sets about building one, of course. . . .

CHAPTER 9: WHAT'S NEXT?

Some fake stories are more fake than others, and we're sorry to say that "And They Say Yelling Never Solves Anything" is nearly entirely make-believe. Renewable energy, and the need for it, is entirely real. And *technically* there is energy stored in sound waves—but a very, very tiny amount. According to one physics source, in order to produce enough power to heat up a single cup of coffee, you would need to yell for 1 year, 7 months, 26 days, 20 hours, 26 minutes, and 40 seconds. There is also no device currently able to store this power, so all that yelling would be in vain. Then again . . . this is today. As for tomorrow—who knows?

Weird and Wacky Science!

Out of all the wild and wacky scientific studies that have been done over the years, there has not yet been one—to our knowledge— that measures the goodness of brownie consumption as it relates to ice cream. Which to us begs the question: Why not?!

BIBLIOGRAPHY

PART 1: IT'S ELEMENTAL

CHAPTER 1: EARTH

The Pit of Despair

AFP. "Turkmenistan Hopes 'Door to Hell' Will Boost Tourism." CTVNews. June 22, 2014. www.ctvnews.ca/sci-tech/turkmenistan-hopes-door-to-hell-will-boost-tourism-1.1880647.

Davies, Elliott. "I Traveled to the Middle of the Desert to See 'The Door to Hell.'" Business Insider. January 26, 2017. www.businessinsider.com/turkmenistan-darvaza-gas-crater-the-door-to-hell-photos-2017-1?r=UK&IR=T.

Geiling, Natasha. "This Hellish Desert Pit Has Been on Fire for More Than 40 Years." Smithsonian.com. May 20, 2014. www.smithsonianmag.com/travel/giant-hole-ground-has-been-fire-more-40-years-180951247.

Gurt, Marat. "Turkmen President Wants to Close." Reuters. April 20, 2010. www.reuters.com/article/us-turkmenistan-crater-odd/turkmen-president-wants-to-close-hells-gate-idUSTRE63J4H120100420.

Nunez, Christina. "Q&A: The First-Ever Expedition to Turkmenistan's 'Door to Hell.'" *National Geographic*. July 17, 2014. https://news.nationalgeographic.com/news/energy/2014/07/140716-door-to-hell-darvaza-crater-george-kourounis-expedition.

They're Maiken a Splash!

AP. "New Volcanic Island Reported in South Pacific Near Tonga." Fox News. November 9, 2006. www.foxnews.com/story/2006/11/09/new-volcanic-island-reported-in-south-pacific-near-tonga.html.

Barone, Jennifer. "Watching the Birth—and Death—of an Island." *Discover.* August 8, 2007. http://discovermagazine.com/2007/aug/watching-birth-and-death-of-an-island.

"Boat Crew Sees Birth of a New Island in South Pacific-Truth! & Outdated!" TruthorFiction.com. May 18, 2016. www.truthorfiction.com/boat-crew-sees-birth-new-island-south-pacific.

Christensen, Brett M. "Floating Volcanic Stones and New Island in the South Pacific." Hoax-Slayer. December 16, 2006. www.hoax-slayer.com/new-pacific-island.shtml.

"EO Newsroom: New Images—New Island and Pumice Raft in the Tongas." Earth Observatory NASA. November 17, 2006. http://web.archive.org/web/20061117034346/http://earthobservatory.nasa.gov/Newsroom/NewImages/images.php3?img_id=17461.

Fransson, Fredrik. "Stone Sea and Volcano." *Fredrik and Crew on* Maiken. August 17, 2006. http://yacht-maiken.blogspot.com/2006/08/stone-sea-and-volcano.html.

Fransson, Fredrik. "Whales and Volcanoes." *Fredrik and Crew on* Maiken. August 12, 2006. http://yacht-maiken.blogspot.com/2006/08/whales-and-volcanoes.html.

"Island." National Geographic Society. October 9, 2012. www.nationalgeographic.org/encyclopedia/island.

"An Island Was Born out of the Ocean Right in Front of Crew Members on Board a Yacht Named *Maiken*." Unbelievable Facts. February 29, 2016. www.unbelievable-facts.com/2016/02/maiken-island.html.

Mikkelson, David. "The *Maiken* and the Birth of an Island." Snopes.com. May 3, 2017. www.snopes.com/fact-check/birth-of-an-island.

A Whirl without a Pool

Andrei, Mihai. "The Eye of the Sahara." ZME Science. May 19, 2016. www.zmescience.com/science/geology/the-eye-of-the-sahara-05102010.

Bartels, Meghan. "Scientists Still Have Questions about the Mysterious Eye of the Sahara." Business Insider. July 12, 2016. www.businessinsider.com/the-eye-of-the-sahara-is-still-a-mystery-2016-7.

NASA Content Administrator. "Richat Structure, Mauritania." NASA. March 23, 2008. www.nasa.gov/multimedia/imagegallery/image_feature_528.html.

"Richat Structure, Mauritania: Image of the Day." Earth Observatory NASA. June 26, 2002. https://earthobservatory.nasa.gov/IOTD/view.php?id=2561.

Zielinski, Sarah. "The Sahara Is Millions of Years Older Than Thought." Smithsonian.com. September 17, 2014. www.smithsonianmag.com/science/sahara-millions-years-older-thought-180952735.

CHAPTER 2: WATER

Ice-capades

"Frost Flowers: A Supercool Ocean Phenomenon." *Kids Discover*. July 31, 2014. www.kidsdiscover.com/quick-reads/frost-flowers-supercool-ocean-phenomenon.

Heimbuch, Jaymi. "8 Strange Ice Formations." MNN—Mother Nature Network. January 5, 2018. www.mnn.com/earth-matters/climate-weather/stories/7-strange-ice-formations.

Israel, Brett. "Photo: Frost Flowers in Bloom on Arctic Sea Ice." Live Science. January 7, 2013. www.livescience.com/31858-frost-flowers-arctic-ocean.html.

Krulwich, Robert. "Suddenly There's a Meadow in the Ocean with 'Flowers' Everywhere." NPR. December 19, 2012. www.npr.org/sections/krulwich/2012/12/17/167469845/suddenly-theres-a-meadow-in-the-ocean-with-flowers-everywhere.

Laskow, Sarah. "The Arctic's Beautiful Frost Flowers Are Home to Millions of Microbes." Grist. December 11, 2012. https://grist.org/article/the-arctics-beautiful-frost-flowers-are-home-to-millions-of-microbes.

Ravilious, Kate. "Mystery of Frost Flower Growth Explained." New Scientist. May 20, 2009. www.newscientist.com/article/dn17166-mystery-of-frost-flower-growth-explained.

The Parting of the Jindo Sea

"Jindo Miracle Sea Road Festival." Imagine Your Korea. Accessed April 6, 2018. http://english.visitkorea.or.kr/enu/ATR/SI_EN_3_2_1.jsp?cid=705394.

"Jindo Sea-Parting Festival, Korea's Moses Miracle, Attracts 80,000 Foreign Tourists." Korea Bizwire. March 25, 2015. http://koreabizwire.com/jindo-sea-parting-festival-koreas-moses-miracle-attracts-80000-foreign-tourists/32296.

Kaushik. "Parting of the Sea in Jindo." Amusing Planet. November 2011. www.amusingplanet.com/2011/11/parting-of-sea-in-jindo.html.

Poon, Linda. "Jindo Sea Parting: Science behind the 'Magic.'" *National Geographic*. April 27, 2013. https://news.nationalgeographic.com/news/2013/13/130426-jindo-sea-parting-festival-korea-red-tides-science-moses.

"When the Sea Parts in South Korea." *Kids Discover*. October 20, 2014. www.kidsdiscover.com/quick-reads/sea-parts-south-korea.

A (Mostly) Lethal Lake

Billock, Jennifer. "The Deadly Lake Where 75 Percent of the World's Lesser Flamingos Are Born." Smithsonian.com. June 14, 2016. www.smithsonianmag.com/travel/flamingos-find-life-among-death-180959265.

"EO Newsroom: New Images—Lake Natron, Tanzania." Earth Observatory NASA. October 1, 2006. https://web.archive.org/web/20061001020850/http://earthobservatory.nasa.gov/Newsroom/NewImages/images.php3?img_id=17239.

Hooper, Rowan. "Deadly Lake Turns Animals into Statues." New Scientist. September 25, 2013. www.newscientist.com/article/mg21929360.100-deadly-lake-turns-animals-into-statues/#.UksfloakolR.

Lallanilla, Marc. "Lake That Turns Animals to Stone? Not Quite." Live Science. October 2, 2013. www.livescience.com/40135-photographer-rick-brandt-lake-natron.html.

Langley, Liz. "Unusual Pictures: 'Calcified' Birds, Bats Found at African Lake." *National Geographic*. October 5, 2013. https://news.nationalgeographic.com/news/2013/10/pictures/131003-calcified-birds-bats-africa-lake-natron-tanzania-animals-science.

Spriggs, Amy. "Eastern Africa: Northern Tanzania, on the Border with Kenya." WWF. Accessed April 7, 2018. www.worldwildlife.org/ecoregions/at0901.

Stromberg, Joseph. "This Alkaline African Lake Turns Animals into Stone." Smithsonian.com. October 2, 2013. www.smithsonianmag.com/science-nature/this-alkaline-african-lake-turns-animals-into-stone-445359.

Subbaraman, Nidhi. "The Bird Mummies of Natron: Lake's Waters Petrify Animals That Fall In." NBCNews.com. October 2, 2013. www.nbcnews.com/science/bird-mummies-natron-lakes-toxic-waters-petrify-animals-fall-8C11322626.

CHAPTER 3: AIR

Krakatau's Loud Last Words

Bagley, Mary. "Krakatoa Volcano: Facts About 1883 Eruption." Live Science. September 14, 2017. www.livescience.com/28186-krakatoa.html.

Bhatia, Aatish. "The Sound So Loud That It Circled the Earth Four Times." *Facts So Romantic*. September 29, 2014. http://nautil.us/blog/the-sound-so-loud-that-it-circled-the-earth-four-times.

History.com Staff. "Krakatoa Erupts." History.com. Updated August 21, 2018. www.history.

com/this-day-in-history/krakatoa-erupts.

McCarthy, Erin. "10 Facts About Krakatoa's 1883 Eruption." Mental Floss. August 27, 2015. http://mentalfloss.com/article/67852/10-facts-about-krakatoas-1883-eruption.

Sturdy, E. W. "The Volcanic Eruption of Krakatoa." *Atlantic*. September 1884. www.theatlantic. com/magazine/archive/1884/09/the-volcanic-eruption-of-krakatoa/376174.

Symons, G. J., ed. *The Eruption of Krakatoa, and Subsequent Phenomena*. Report of the Krakatoa Committee of the Royal Society. London: Trübner, 1888. https://books. google.com/books?id=Vk8PAAAAYAAJ&printsec=frontcover&source=gbs_ge_ summary_r&cad=0#v=onepage&q&f=false.

Williams, Jack. "The Epic Volcano Eruption That Led to the 'Year without a Summer.'" *Washington Post*. June 10, 2016. www.washingtonpost.com/news/capital-weather-gang/ wp/2015/04/24/the-epic-volcano-eruption-that-led-to-the-year-without-a-summer.

Winchester, Simon. *Krakatoa: The Day the World Exploded*: August 27, 1883. New York: Harper Perennial, 2005.

Windmills to the Rescue

"The Congo Basin Forest." Global Forest Atlas. Accessed October 9, 2018. https:// globalforestatlas.yale.edu/region/congo.

Gottlieb, Paul. "Numbers Vary on Turbine Electrical Generation: Intent Not Power Production, Port Angeles City Says." *Peninsula Daily News*. December 9, 2016. www.peninsuladailynews. com/news/wind-turbines-generating-regret-100000-turbines-to-create-1-50-in- electricity-monthly.

Lakshmanan, Lak, and Matthew Feigal. "Using Google Cloud Machine Learning to Manage Dutch Weather Conditions." *Google Cloud*. April 1, 2017. https://cloud.google.com/blog/ products/gcp/using-google-cloud-machine-learning-to-manage-dutch-weather-conditions.

"The Netherlands Travel." Lonely Planet. Accessed October 9, 2018. www.lonelyplanet.com/ the-netherlands.

Wiltz, Chris. "9 of the Best Fake Gadgets of 2017." Design News. April 4, 2017. www. designnews.com/consumer-electronics/9-best-fake-gadgets-2017/161481574656565.

Firenado!

Finneran, Michael. "Fire-Breathing Storm Systems." NASA. October 19, 2010. www.nasa.gov/topics/earth/features/pyrocb.html.

Fromm, M., D. T. Lindsey, R. Servranckx, G. Yue, T. Trickl, R. Sica, P. Doucet, and S. Godin-Beekmann. "The Untold Story of Pyrocumulonimbus." *Bulletin of the American Meteorological Society* 91 (2010): 1193–1210. https://doi.org/10.1175/2010BAMS3004.1.

Harvey, Chelsea. "Here's What We Know about Wildfires and Climate Change." *Scientific American*. October 13, 2017. www.scientificamerican.com/article/heres-what-we-know-about-wildfires-and-climate-change.

Lallanilla, Marc. "Whirling Flames: How Fire Tornadoes Work." Live Science. May 16, 2014. www.livescience.com/45676-what-is-a-firenado.html.

Nairn, Jessica. "Researchers Document World-First Fire Tornado." ABC News. November 19, 2012. www.abc.net.au/news/2012-11-19/researchers-document-world-first-fire-tornado/4380252.

Specktor, Brandon. "What Are Pyrocumulus Clouds? California Fires Spawn Eerie Formations." Live Science. December 12, 2017. www.livescience.com/61167-what-are-pyrocumulus-clouds.html.

PART 2: SENSATIONAL SCIENCE

CHAPTER 4: UNCANNY CHEMISTRY

Quite a Sweet Story!

"10 Ideas for Flavoring Water Kefir." Cultures for Health. 2017. www.culturesforhealth.com/learn/water-kefir/ten-ways-to-flavor-water-kefir.

"13 Surprising Benefits of Papaya (Pawpaw)." Organic Facts. August 10, 2018. www.organicfacts.net/health-benefits/fruit/health-benefits-of-papaya.html.

Egbinola, Christiana Ndidi, and Amobichukwu Chukwudi Amanambu. "Groundwater Contamination in Ibadan, South-West Nigeria." National Center for Biotechnology Information, U.S. National Library of Medicine, National Institute of Health. August 20, 2014. www.ncbi.nlm.nih.gov/pmc/articles/PMC4447718.

"Home Page." Yeshua Papaya Farms. 2015. Accessed October 9, 2018. http://yeshuapapayafarms.com.ng.

Hufstader, Chris. "Six Ways to Fix Up a Well and Get Clean Water." *First Person Blog*. May 20, 2016. https://firstperson.oxfamamerica.org/2016/05/six-ways-to-fix-up-a-well-and-get-clean-water.

"Improving the Wells Improves Community Health in Flood-Prone Parts of El Salvador." Oxfam International. Accessed April 9, 2018. www.oxfam.org/en/countries/improving-wells-improves-community-health-flood-prone-parts-el-salvador.

McPhillips, Deidre. "10 Countries with the Worst Drinking Water." *U.S. News & World Report*. July 14, 2017. www.usnews.com/news/best-countries/slideshows/10-countries-with-the-worst-water-supply?slide=9.

"Nigeria." World Health Organization (WHO). 2015. www.who.int/water_sanitation_health/monitoring/investments/nigeria-10-nov.pdf.

Pariona, Amber. "Top Papaya Producing Countries in the World." WorldAtlas. April 25, 2017. www.worldatlas.com/articles/top-papaya-producing-countries-in-the-world.html.

Spritzler, Franziska. "8 Evidence-Based Health Benefits of Papaya." Healthline. Accessed April 9, 2018. www.healthline.com/nutrition/8-proven-papaya-benefits.

"Water Crisis—Learn About the Global Water Crisis." Water.org. Accessed April 9, 2018. https://water.org/our-impact/water-crisis.

"Water Kefir FAQ: Secondary Ferments & Flavoring." Yemoos Nourishing Cultures. Accessed April 9, 2018. www.yemoos.com/pages/water-kefir-faq-secondary-ferments-flavoring.

Here Be Giants

Amos, Jonathan. "Naica's Crystal Caves Hold Long-Dormant Life." BBC News. February 18, 2017. www.bbc.com/news/science-environment-39013829.

Borenstein, Seth. "Scientists Find 50,000-Year-Old Microbes in Mexican Caves." *Boston Globe*. February 18, 2017. www.bostonglobe.com/metro/2017/02/18/scientists-find-year-old-microbes-mexican-caves/34CzW361KG9yavD8xB3ZMN/story.html.

Jaggard, Victoria. "Weird Life Found Trapped in Giant Underground Crystals." *National Geographic*. February 17, 2017. https://news.nationalgeographic.com/2017/02/crystal-caves-mine-microbes-mexico-boston-aaas-aliens-science.

Lovgren, Stefan. "Giant Crystal Cave's Mystery Solved." *National Geographic*. April 6, 2007. https://news.nationalgeographic.com/news/2007/04/070406-giant-crystals_2.html.

Nace, Trevor. "50,000-Year-Old 'Super Life' Discovered Says Head of NASA Astrobiology." *Forbes*. February 28, 2017. www.forbes.com/sites/trevornace/2017/02/27/50000-year-old-super-life-discovered-in-mexico-cave/#20ab88659c18.

Pappas, Stephanie. "Microbes in Glittering Cave Revived after 10,000 Years, Scientists Say." CBS News. February 24, 2017. www.cbsnews.com/news/microbes-in-glittering-cave-revived-after-10000-years.

Shea, Neil. "Crystal Palace." *National Geographic*, November 2008, 65–77. ProQuest Research Library (200961122).

Stewart, Iain. "A Rare Glimpse of the Cave of Crystals." BBC News. January 19, 2010. http://news.bbc.co.uk/2/hi/science/nature/8466493.stm.

Zajac, Linda. "Breathtaking CRYSTALS: Secrets in the Naica Mine." *Muse*, January 2016, 9–12. ProQuest Research Library (1784560446).

Are You Boared Yet?

Andrews, Travis M. "Thousands of Radioactive Boars Are Overrunning Farmland in Fukushima." *Washington Post*. April 11, 2016. www.washingtonpost.com/news/morning-mix/wp/2016/04/11/thousands-of-radioactive-boars-are-overrunning-farmland-in-fukushima/?utm_term=.424fab33cfb0.

Baird, Sarah. "Attack of the (Radioactive) Wild Boars." Outside Online. December 27, 2016. www.outsideonline.com/2141891/attack-radioactive-wild-boars.

Dearden, Lizzie. "Radioactive Wild Boars Are Running Wild around Fukushima." *Independent*. March 11, 2017. www.independent.co.uk/news/world/asia/japan-earthquake-tsunami-2011-tohoku-wild-boars-radioactive-fukushima-nuclear-accident-meltdown-a7624401.html.

Freytas-tamura, Kimiko De. "Radioactive Boars in Fukushima Thwart Residents' Plans to Return Home." *New York Times*. March 9, 2017. www.nytimes.com/2017/03/09/world/asia/radioactive-boars-in-fukushima-thwart-residents-plans-to-return-home.html.

Kasai, Teppei. "Wild Boars Offer Challenge for Homecomers in Radiation-Hit Fukushima." Reuters. March 9, 2017. www.reuters.com/article/us-japan-fukushima-wild-boars/wild-boars-offer-challenge-for-homecomers-in-radiation-hit-fukushima-idUSKBN16G079.

Taylor, Alan. "The Wild Boars of Fukushima." Atlantic. March 9, 2017. www.theatlantic.com/photo/2017/03/the-wild-boars-of-fukushima/519066.

CHAPTER 5: FREAKY PHYSICS

The Beests on the Beach

Architectural Digest. "Theo Jansen's Strandbeests Walk New England Beaches." September 16, 2015. www.architecturaldigest.com/story/theo-jansen-strandbeest-comes-to-massachusetts.

Campion, Sebastian. "Interview with Theo Jansen." Artificial. October 21, 2005. www.artificial.dk/articles/theojansen.htm.

Dawson, Michael R. W., Brian Dupuis, and Michael Wilson. "5.13.2 Strandbeest." In *From Bricks to Brains: The Embodied Cognitive Science of LEGO Robots*, 135. Athabasca University Press, 2014. https://books.google.com/books?id=fSUOc48GxGcC&pg=PA135#v=onepage&q&f=false.

Frazier, Ian. "The March of the Strandbeests." *New Yorker.* June 19, 2017. www.newyorker.com/magazine/2011/09/05/the-march-of-the-strandbeests.

Jansen, Theo. "My Creations, a New Form of Life." Filmed March 2007 at TED2007. TED Video, 8:10. www.ted.com/talks/theo_jansen_creates_new_creatures.

Macdonald, Fiona. "Theo Jansen's Strandbeests: Wind-Powered Skeletons." BBC News. December 4, 2014. www.bbc.com/culture/story/20141204-skeletons-that-walk-on-the-wind.

Meis, Morgan. "Still Alive." *The Smart Set*. May 18, 2015. https://thesmartset.com/still-alive-theo-jansen-strandbeests.

"Theo Jansen's Strandbeest." Accessed April 8, 2018. www.strandbeest.com.

"Theo Jansen's Strandbeests: Crane Beach, Ipswich MA." Produced by Ipswich Community Access Media (ICAM), August 26, 2015. YouTube video, 4:44. www.youtube.com/watch?v=0jlGTcfnvPw.

Fidget Spinners' Revenge

Allain, Rhett. "Want to Know How Long a Fidget Spinner Spins? Get a Laser and Some Physics." *Wired*. June 3, 2017. www.wired.com/2017/05/the-phyiscs-of-fidget-spinners.

Bogost, Ian. "The Fidget Spinner Explains the World." *Atlantic*. May 12, 2017. www.theatlantic.com/technology/archive/2017/05/the-fidget-spinner-explains-the-world/526521.

Calfas, Jennifer. "Fidget Spinners: What Are They? Where Can I Buy?" *Time*. May 4, 2017. http://time.com/money/4766890/fidget-spinners-what-to-know.

Hebert, Kayla. "Fact and Fiction about the Fidget Spinner." WeHaveKids. July 7, 2017. https://wehavekids.com/parenting/The-Fidget-Spinner-Grapevine.

Huppke, Rex. "Are Fidget Spinners a Threat to America? Yes. Yes, They Are." *Chicago Tribune*. May 3, 2017. www.chicagotribune.com/news/opinion/huppke/ct-fidget-spinners-schools-huppke-20170501-story.html.

Jacobs, Jeff. "Fidget Spinners Disrupt Earth's Gravity." LinkedIn. July 7, 2017. www.linkedin.com/pulse/fidget-spinners-disrupt-earths-gravity-jeff-jacobs.

Jolina. "Fidget Spinners May Cause Earthquake, Affects Earth's Center of Gravity Says Fake News." Hall of Fame Magazine. May 25, 2017. www.hofmag.com/fidget-spinners-may-cause-earthquake/220452.

Mikkelson, David. "FACT CHECK: Physicist Warns That Fidget Spinners Could Affect Earth's Center of Gravity?" Snopes.com. May 23, 2017. www.snopes.com/fact-check/fidget-spinners-affect-gravity.

"Search Results." Guinness World Records. Accessed May 3, 2018. www.guinnessworldrecords.com/search?term=fidget%2Bspinner.

Willingham, AJ. "All Your Questions about Fidget Spinners, Answered." CNN. May 5, 2017. www.cnn.com/2017/05/05/health/fidget-spinners-what-is-trnd/index.html.

Any Body Can Live Forever!

"Bio Urn, Tree Burial, Cremation Tree." The Living Urn. Accessed April 6, 2018. www.thelivingurn.com.

Bios Urn. "The Biodegradable Urn Designed to Grow a Tree." Bios Urn. July 30, 2015. https://urnabios.com.

Erizanu, Paula. "Organic Burial Pod Turns Your Body into a Tree." CNN. January 11, 2018. www.cnn.com/2017/05/03/world/eco-solutions-capsula-mundi/index.html.

"Frequently Asked Questions." LifeGem. Accessed April 6, 2018. www.lifegem.com/LifeGemFAQ.php.

"From the Ashes: 3 Companies That'll Turn Cremains into a Tree." Modern Farmer. September 28, 2017. https://modernfarmer.com/2016/04/ashes-ashes-turn-cremains-tree.

CHAPTER 6: SURPRISING SPACE

Hello, Goodbye, Whoosh!

"A Single Photon Is the First Object to Be Teleported from the Ground to an Orbiting Satellite." *MIT Technology Review*. July 11, 2017. www.technologyreview.com/s/608252/first-object-teleported-from-earth-to-orbit.

Datta, Bianca. "Scientists 'Teleport' Photons into Space for the First Time." PBS. July 14, 2017. www.pbs.org/wgbh/nova/next/space/scientists-teleport-photons-into-space-for-the-first-time.

"Einstein's 'Spooky Action at a Distance' Paradox Older Than Thought." *MIT Technology Review*. October 22, 2012. www.technologyreview.com/s/427174/einsteins-spooky-action-at-a-distance-paradox-older-than-thought.

Emspak, Jesse. "Chinese Scientists Just Set the Record for the Farthest Quantum Teleportation." Space.com. November 2, 2017. www.space.com/37506-quantum-teleportation-record-shattered.html.

Lucy, Michael. "What 'Teleporting' a Photon to Space Means." Cosmos. July 12, 2017. https://cosmosmagazine.com/physics/chinese-scientists-teleport-a-photon-to-space.

Mosher, Dave. "China Has Pulled Off a 'Profound' Feat of Teleportation That May Help It 'Dominate the Way the World Works.'" Business Insider. July 20, 2017. www.businessinsider.com/china-teleportation-space-quantum-internet-2017-7.

Siegfried, Tom. "Entanglement Is Spooky, but Not Action at a Distance." Science News. January 27, 2016. www.sciencenews.org/blog/context/entanglement-spooky-not-action-distance.

Whitley-Berry, Victoria. "Beam Me Up, Scotty . . . Sort Of. Chinese Scientists 'Teleport' Photon to Space." NPR. July 14, 2017. www.npr.org/2017/07/14/537174817/scientists-teleport-a-photon-into-space.

Things You Think About When the Sky Is Falling

Ellington, M. J. "A Star Fell on Sylacauga: '54 Meteorite Struck Home, Woman, Changed Lives." *Decatur Daily News*. November 30, 2006. http://archive.decaturdaily.com/decaturdaily/news/061130/meteorite.shtml.

Eschner, Kat. "For the Only Person Ever Hit by a Meteorite, the Real Trouble Began Later." Smithsonian.com. November 30, 2016. www.smithsonianmag.com/smart-news/only-person-ever-hit-meteorite-real-trouble-began-later-180961238.

"FAQ—Meteoroids/Meteorites." Planetary Science Institute. May 31, 2018. www.psi.edu/epo/faq/meteor.html.

Hall, John C. "Hodges Meteorite Strike (Sylacauga Aerolite)." Encyclopedia of Alabama. November 22, 2016. www.encyclopediaofalabama.org/article/h-1280.

"HubbleSite—Reference Desk—FAQs." HubbleSite. Accessed April 7, 2018. http://hubblesite.org/reference_desk/faq/answer.php.id=22&cat=solarsystem.

Mathewson, Samantha. "How Often Do Meteorites Hit the Earth?" Space.com. August 10, 2016. www.space.com/33695-thousands-meteorites-litter-earth-unpredictable-collisions.html.

Nobel, Justin. "The True Story of History's Only Known Meteorite Victim." *National Geographic*. November 30, 2016. https://news.nationalgeographic.com/news/2013/02/130220-russia-meteorite-ann-hodges-science-space-hit.

Plait, Phil. "60 Years Ago Today, a Human Was Hit by a Meteorite." *Bad Astronomy*. November 30, 2014. www.slate.com/blogs/bad_astronomy/2014/11/30/sylacauga_meteorite_60th_anniversary_of_a_human_hit_by_a_space_rock.html.

Helloooo! Anyone Else Out There?

"Broadcasting a Message." SETI Institute. Accessed April 8, 2018. www.seti.org/seti-institute/project/details/broadcasting-message.

Cofield, Calla. "Mysterious Radio Blasts from a Distant Galaxy Draw Attention of Alien Hunters." Space.com. January 11, 2018. www.space.com/39358-breakthrough-listen-radio-burst-not-aliens.html.

Garber, Steve. "SETI: The Search for ExtraTerrestrial Intelligence." NASA. September 29, 2014. https://history.nasa.gov/seti.html.

Griffin, Andrew. "Strange Messages Coming from the Stars Are 'Probably' from Aliens, Scientists Say." *Independent*. October 24, 2016. www.independent.co.uk/news/science/aliens-proof-evidence-facts-stars-scientists-extraterrestrial-life-et-intelligence-a7377716.html.

"History of the SETI Institute." SETI Institute. Accessed September 17, 2018. www.seti.org/history-seti-institute.

Kawa, Barry. "The 'Wow!' Signal." Big Ear Radio Observatory. September 6, 2006. http://bigear.org/wow.htm.

Morris, Chris. "Five Things You Should Know About the New Planet Ross 128." *Fortune*. November 15, 2017. http://fortune.com/2017/11/15/five-things-to-know-about-ross-128.

Redd, Nola Taylor. "Red Dwarfs: The Most Common and Longest-Lived Stars." Space.com. December 21, 2016. www.space.com/23772-red-dwarf-stars.html.

"SETI: The Search for Extra-terrestrial Intelligence." IOP—Institute of Physics. Accessed April 8, 2018. www.iop.org/resources/topic/archive/seti/index.html.

Wall, Mike. "Weird Radio Signals Detected from Nearby Red Dwarf Star." Space.com. November 2, 2017. www.space.com/37516-strange-radio-signals-red-dwarf-star.html.

Ward, Tom. "The 40-Year Old Mystery of the 'Wow!' Signal Was Just Solved." Futurism. June 7, 2017. https://futurism.com/the-40-year-old-mystery-of-the-wow-signal-was-just-solved.

PART 3: SCIENCE IN ACTION

CHAPTER 7: AMAZING

You Can Call Me "Agent Spywing"

Brown, Daniel. "Here's How Military Dolphins Are Used to Protect US Nukes and Spot Enemy Mines." Business Insider. May 3, 2017. www.businessinsider.com/these-9-photos-show-how-navy-trains-dolphins-detect-mines-2017-5#-the-navy-has-some-weapons-that-are-most-decidedly-low-tech-dolphins-3.

Corrigan, Fintan. "How Do Drones Work and What Is Drone Technology." DroneZon. August 29, 2018. www.dronezon.com/learn-about-drones-quadcopters/what-is-drone-technology-or-how-does-drone-technology-work.

Earls, Alan, Sharon Shea, and Ivy Wigmore. "What Is Drone (Unmanned Aerial Vehicle, UAV)?—Definition from WhatIs.com." IoT Agenda. October 2016. https://internetofthingsagenda.techtarget.com/definition/drone.

Essary, Tyler. "French Air Force Trains Eagles to Hunt Drones." *Time*. February 17, 2017. http://time.com/4675164/drone-hunting-eagles.

Hardy, Catherine. "Where Eagles Dare: France Trains Birds to Bring down Drones." Euronews. February 16, 2017. www.euronews.com/2017/02/16/where-eagles-dare-france-trains-birds-to-bring-down-drones.

Selk, Avi. "Terrorists Are Building Drones. France Is Destroying Them with Eagles." *Washington Post.* February 21, 2017. www.washingtonpost.com/news/worldviews/wp/2017/02/21/terrorists-are-building-drones-france-is-destroying-them-with-eagles.

Waxman, Olivia B. "That Time the CIA Tried to Train Cats to Be Spies." *Time.* July 26, 2017. http://time.com/4868642/cia-anniversary-national-security-act-cats.

Later, Gator!

Clark, Joe. "10-Year-Old Girl Describes Fighting off 8-foot Alligator in Florida Waters." NBC4 WCMH-TV Columbus. May 9, 2017. www.nbc4i.com/news/u-s-world/10-year-old-girl-describes-fighting-off-8-foot-alligator-in-florida-waters/1065007676.

Hill, Erin. "10-Year-Old Girl Who Fought Off Alligator That Attacked Her Speaks Out: 'I Tried Hitting It to Release Me.'" *People.* May 8, 2017. https://people.com/human-interest/10-year-old-girl-fought-off-alligator-that-attacked-speaks-out.

Johnson, Alex. "10-Year-Old Florida Girl Pries Leg from Alligator's Mouth, Says, 'I Knew What to Do.'" NBC News. May 9, 2017. www.nbcnews.com/news/us-news/10-year-old-florida-girl-pries-leg-alligator-s-mouth-n756676.

"10-year-old Alligator Bite Victim Says Nose Poke Stopped Attack." CBS News. May 9, 2017. www.cbsnews.com/news/alligator-bite-victim-nose-poke-gatorland-moss-park-florida.

Walsh, S. M. "Juliana Ossa: 5 Fast Facts You Need to Know." Heavy. May 9, 2017. https://heavy.com/news/2017/05/juliana-ossa-girl-fights-off-alligator-gator-orlando-florida.

Tesla's "Death Ray" Disaster

History.com Editors. "Nikola Tesla." History.com. November 9, 2009. www.history.com/topics/inventions/nikola-tesla.

Hogenboom, Melissa. "In Siberia in 1908, a Huge Explosion Came out of Nowhere." BBC News. July 7, 2016. www.bbc.com/earth/story/20160706-in-siberia-in-1908-a-huge-explosion-came-out-of-nowhere.

Jay, Paul. "The Tunguska Event." CBC News. June 30, 2008. www.cbc.ca/news/technology/the-tunguska-event-1.742329.

Science@NASA. "The Tunguska Impact—100 Years Later." NASA. June 30, 2008. https://science.nasa.gov/science-news/science-at-nasa/2008/30jun_tunguska.

"The Tunguska Blast: Tesla's Death Ray." Theunredacted.com. March 10, 2016. https://theunredacted.com/the-tunguska-blast-teslas-death-ray.

CHAPTER 8: UNBELIEVABLE

Death Comes from the Deep

"Artifacts—Staten Island Ferry Disaster Memorial Museum." Super Fun Co. Accessed April 10, 2018. www.sioctopusdisaster.com/artifacts.html.

Associated Press in New York. "New York Monument Honors Victims of Giant Octopus Attack That Never Occurred." *Guardian*. October 1, 2016. www.theguardian.com/us-news/2016/oct/01/new-york-staten-island-ferry-octopus-attack-fake-monument.

"Giant Squid." *National Geographic*. Accessed April 10, 2018. www.nationalgeographic.com/animals/invertebrates/g/giant-squid.

Gibson, Joe. "Second Giant Sea Creature Washes Ashore Along Santa Monica Coastline—Alarms Sound over Radioactive Gigantism." LBT Today. January 13, 2018. www.lightlybraisedturnip.com/giant-squid-in-california.

Levith, Will. "Artist Tricks New York City Tourists with Fake Monument Depicting Squid Disaster in Staten Island." RealClearLife. October 4, 2016. www.realclearlife.com/travel/artist-tricks-new-york-city-tourists-with-fake-monument-depicting-squid-disaster-in-staten-island/#1.

Linge, Mary Kay. "Artist Fools Tourists with Monument to Giant-Octopus Attack on Staten Island Ferry." *New York Post*. September 25, 2016. https://nypost.com/2016/09/25/artist-fools-tourists-with-monument-to-giant-octopus-attack-on-staten-island-ferry.

Roper, Clyde, and Ocean Portal Team. "Giant Squid." Ocean Portal | Smithsonian. April 2018. https://ocean.si.edu/ocean-life/invertebrates/giant-squid.

"Staten Island Ferry Disaster Memorial." Super Fun Co. Accessed April 10, 2018. www.sioctopusdisaster.com/memorial.html.

"The Staten Island Ferry." The Staten Island Ferry Information and History. Accessed April 10, 2018. www.siferry.com.

"Staten Island Ferry." Wastewater Treatment Process. Accessed April 10, 2018. www.nyc.gov/

html/dot/html/ferrybus/staten-island-ferry.shtml.

Walker, Matt. "Earth—The 27-Metre-Long Giant Sea Monster." BBC News. May 27, 2016. www.
bbc.com/earth/story/20160524-the-27-metre-long-giant-sea-monster.

Yong, Ed. "How Big Are the Biggest Squid, Whales, Sharks, Jellyfish?" *National Geographic*.
January 13, 2015. www.nationalgeographic.com/science/phenomena/2015/01/13/how-
big-are-the-biggest-squid-whales-sharks-jellyfish.

Your Dinner Is in the Printer, Dear!

"3D Food Printing: A Promising Innovation Making Its Way to Consumers." 3D FilaPrints
Blog. April 22, 2016. http://shop.3dfilaprint.com/blog/2016/04/22/3d-food-printing-a-
promising-innovation-making-its-way-to-consumers.

Bean, Quincy, and Kirt Costello. "3D Printing In Zero-G Technology Demonstration." NASA.
December 6, 2017. www.nasa.gov/mission_pages/station/research/experiments/1115.
html.

Chang, Lulu. "At This Restaurant the Chef Is a 3D Printer." Digital Trends. August 4, 2016.
www.digitaltrends.com/cool-tech/food-ink-3d-printing.

Chow, Denise. "NASA Funds 3D Pizza Printer." Space.com. March 8, 2016. www.space.
com/21250-nasa-3d-food-printer-pizza.html.

Duley, Jason. "3D Food Printer in Space." NASA. September 2, 2015. https://open.nasa.gov/
innovation-space/3d-food-printer-in-space.

Dunbar, Brian. "3D Printing: Food in Space." NASA. July 28, 2013. www.nasa.gov/directorates/
spacetech/home/feature_3d_food.html.

Fussell, Sidney. "This Company Is Creating Incredible 3D Printed Food You Can Eat." Business
Insider. April 8, 2016. www.businessinsider.com/3d-printed-food-foodini-2016-4.

Garfield, Leanna. "This Robot Can 3D-Print and Bake a Pizza in Six Minutes." Business Insider.
March 4, 2017. www.businessinsider.com/beehex-pizza-3d-printer-2017-3.

Gohd, Chelsea. "NASA Astronauts Can Now 3D-Print Pizzas in Space." Futurism. March 7, 2017.
https://futurism.com/nasa-astronauts-can-now-3d-print-pizzas-in-space.

"The History of 3D Printing." All That 3D. Accessed September 26, 2018. www.allthat3d.
com/3d-printing-history.

Molitch-Hou, Michael. "The Future of Building and 3D Printing in Space." Engineering.com.
March 10, 2017. www.engineering.com/3DPrinting/3DPrintingArticles/ArticleID/14481/
The-Future-of-Building-and-3D-Printing-in-Space.aspx.

Olson, Maryanne. "A Brief History of 3D Printing." AIO Robotcs. September 13, 2016. www.
zeus.aiorobotics.com/single-post/2016/09/13/A-Brief-History-of-3D-Printing.

"Print Pizza in Any Shape You Want." Fine Dining Lovers. March 3, 2017. www.
finedininglovers.com/blog/news-trends/chef-3d.

Prisco, Jacopo. "'Foodini' Machine Lets You Print Edible Burgers, Pizza." CNN. December 31,
2014. www.cnn.com/2014/11/06/tech/innovation/foodini-machine-print-food/index.
html.

Sandle, Tim. "3D Printing Could Solve Organ Transplant Shortage." Digital Journal. August 3,
2017. www.digitaljournal.com/tech-and-science/science/3d-printing-could-solve-organ-
transplant-shortage/article/499166.

"What Is 3D Printing? How Does a 3D Printer Work? Learn 3D Printing." 3D Printing.
September 10, 2018. https://3dprinting.com/what-is-3d-printing.

Yoders, Jeff. "What Materials Are Used in 3D Printing? Not Just Plastic [Updated]." *Redshift
by Autodesk*. May 3, 2018. www.autodesk.com/redshift/what-materials-are-used-in-3d-
printing.

That's What We Call a One-Man Operation

"Appendicitis." Mayo Clinic. July 6, 2018. www.mayoclinic.org/diseases-conditions/
appendicitis/symptoms-causes/syc-20369543.

"Dr. Leonid Rogozov Operating Himself to Remove His Appendix in Antarctica, 1961." Rare
Historical Photos. October 14, 2017. https://rarehistoricalphotos.com/leonid-rogozov-
appendix-1961.

Lentati, Sara. "The Man Who Cut out His Own Appendix." BBC News. May 5, 2015. www.bbc.
com/news/magazine-32481442.

Madrigal, Alexis C. "Antarctica, 1961: A Soviet Surgeon Has to Remove His Own Appendix."
Atlantic. March 14, 2011. www.theatlantic.com/technology/archive/2011/03/antarctica-
1961-a-soviet-surgeon-has-to-remove-his-own-appendix/72445.

"That Self-Appendectomy." Amundsen-Scott South Pole Station. Accessed April 11, 2018. www.
southpolestation.com/trivia/igy1/appendix.html.

CHAPTER 9: WHAT'S NEXT?

If You Dream It, You Can . . . See It?!

AFP. "Japanese Scientists Can Read Dreams in Breakthrough with MRI Scans." *South China Morning Post*. April 7, 2013. www.scmp.com/lifestyle/technology/article/1208614/japanese-scientists-can-read-dreams-breakthrough-mri-scans.

Akst, Jef. "Decoding Dreams." *Scientist*. January 1, 2013. www.the-scientist.com/notebook/decoding-dreams-39990.

Anwar, Yasmin. "Scientists Use Brain Imaging to Reveal the Movies in Our Mind." Berkeley News. March 24, 2016. http://news.berkeley.edu/2011/09/22/brain-movies.

DreamsCloud. "Can We Turn Our Dreams into Watchable Movies?" Huffington Post. December 7, 2017. www.huffingtonpost.com/dreamscloud/can-we-turn-our-dreams-in_b_9152612.html.

Kamitani, Yukiyasu, and Frank Tong. "Decoding the Visual and Subjective Contents of the Human Brain." *Nature Neuroscience* 8: 679–685 (2005). www.nature.com/articles/nn1444.

Kamitani, Yukiyasu. E-mail interview by author Ammi-Joan Paquette. August 10, 2018.

Ketler, Alanna. "Scientists Are Learning to Record Your Dreams & Play Them Back to You." Collective Evolution. January 19, 2016. www.collective-evolution.com/2016/01/20/scientists-are-learning-to-record-your-dreams-play-them-back-to-you.

Morelle, Rebecca. "Scientists 'Read Dreams' Using Brain Scans." BBC News. April 4, 2013. www.bbc.com/news/science-environment-22031074.

Nelson, Bryan. "Scientists Learn How to Record Your Dreams and Play Them Back to You." MNN—Mother Nature Network. June 23, 2017. www.mnn.com/green-tech/research-innovations/stories/scientists-learn-how-to-record-your-dreams-and-play-them.

Robertson, Adi. "Scientists Turn Dreams into Eerie Short Films with an MRI Scan." Verge. April 4, 2013. www.theverge.com/2013/4/4/4184728/scientists-decode-dreams-with-mri-scan.

Stromberg, Joseph. "Scientists Figure Out What You See While You're Dreaming." Smithsonian.com. April 4, 2013. www.smithsonianmag.com/science-nature/scientists-figure-out-what-you-see-while-youre-dreaming-15553304.

And They Say Yelling Never Solves Anything

"How Long Would You Have to Yell to Heat a Cup of Coffee?" PhysicsCentral. Accessed April 12, 2018. www.physicscentral.com/explore/poster-coffee.cfm.

"Japan Country Profile." BBC News. February 20, 2018. www.bbc.com/news/world-asia-pacific-14918801.

Lonelynight. "8 Countries with No Natural Resource But, Thrive to Become World Major Exporters—Off-Topic Discussion." GameSpot. 2013. www.gamespot.com/forums/offtopic-discussion-314159273/8-countries-with-no-natural-resource-but-thrive-to-29364331.

Lumb, David. "Singapore Bans Additional Cars to Keep Traffic from Getting Worse." Engadget. October 23, 2017. www.engadget.com/2017/10/23/singapore-bans-additional-cars-to-keep-traffic-from-getting-wors.

"Potential Energy." The Physics Classroom. Accessed April 12, 2018. www.physicsclassroom.com/class/energy/Lesson-1/Potential-Energy.

Rouse, Margaret. "What Is Kinetic Energy?—Definition from WhatIs.com." WhatIs.com. December 2007. https://whatis.techtarget.com/definition/kinetic-energy.

"TomTom Traffic Index." Tomtom. 2016. www.tomtom.com/en_gb/trafficindex/city/singapore.

I, Robot. I, Worm.

Altun, Z. F., and Hall D. H. "Introduction to C. Elegans Anatomy." WormAtlas. 2009. https://doi.org/10.3908/wormatlas.1.1.

Black, Lucy. "A Worm's Mind in a Lego Body." I Programmer. November 16, 2014. www.i-programmer.info/news/105-artificial-intelligence/7985-a-worms-mind-in-a-lego-body.html.

Fessenden, Marissa. "We've Put a Worm's Mind in a Lego Robot's Body." Smithsonian.com. November 19, 2014. www.smithsonianmag.com/smart-news/weve-put-worms-mind-lego-robot-body-180953399.

"Getting Started." OpenWorm. Accessed April 13, 2018. http://openworm.org/getting_started.html.

"A History and Pre-History of OpenWorm." OpenWorm. Accessed April 13, 2018. http://docs. openworm.org/en/latest/fullhistory.

Kim, Brenda Kelley. "A Worm Brain in a Robot?" LabRoots. January 15, 2018. www.labroots. com/trending/neuroscience/7825/worm-brain-robot.

MacDonald, Fiona. "Scientists Put a Worm Brain in a Lego Robot Body—And It Worked." ScienceAlert. December 11, 2017. www.sciencealert.com/scientists-put-worm-brain-in-lego-robot-openworm-connectome.

PHOTOGRAPH CREDITS

The authors would like to thank the following for granting permission to reproduce the images used in this book:

page 1 © Patrick Orton/Getty Images
page 2 TUBS/Wikimedia Commons
page 3 © Lockenes/Shutterstock
page 4 Tormod Sandtorv (tormods)/Flickr
page 5 © Bruno D'Amicis/Nature Picture Library/Alamy Stock Photo
page 6 mapswire.com
page 7 © Fredrik Fransson
page 9 © Fredrik Fransson
page 11 © Fredrik Fransson
page 12 mapswire.com
page 13 NASA/Wikimedia Commons
page 15 ESA/Wikimedia Commons
page 16 © Dave Brosha Photography/Aurora Photos/Alamy Stock Photo
page 17 © Janne Kahila
page 18 © Matthias Wietz
page 20 © Matthias Wietz
page 21 © PeterHermesFurian/iStockPhoto LP
page 22 © Yonhap News/YNA/Newscom
page 23 © markhanna/RooM the Agency/Alamy Stock Photo
page 24 Piotrus/Wikimedia Commons
page 26 mapswire.com
page 27 © Nigel Pavitt/John Warburton-Lee Photography/Alamy Stock Photo
page 28 Christoph Strässler (christoph_straessler)/Flickr
page 31 Lithograph: Parker & Coward, Britain/Wikimedia Commons
page 32 ChrisDHDR/Wikimedia Commons
page 34 Edvard Munch/Wikimedia Commons
page 36 Alphathon/Wikimedia Commons
page 37 Gargi Biswas 25/Wikimedia Commons
page 38 © Google
page 39 © zorazhuang/iStockPhoto LP
page 41 Jan van Rooyen/Wikimedia Commons
page 42 Dake and RicHard-59/Wikimedia Commons

INDEX

Page numbers in *italics* refer to illustrations.

Darvaza Crater
    as "Door to Hell," 3, *3*
    gas burning in, 3–4
    at twilight, *4*
death, 72. *See also* after-death remains;
        postmortem
    Tesla not creating ray of, 154
debris, 86
decibels
    barographs and Krakatau, 34–35
    sound measurement in, *33*, 33–34,
        34
Denver Institute of Science, 68
diamonds, 73, *73*
disasters
    Darvaza Crater, *3*, 3–4, *4*
    Japan nuclear power plant and,
        58, 58–59, *59*
    Krakatau volcano, *31*, 31–35, *32*
    reactions and prevention of, 5
    responses to, 5
Drake, Frank, 90
dreams
    journaling of, 132
    reading of, *130*, 130–31
    sleeping brain and, 128–29
drones
    eagles attacking, 98
    eagles born on, 97
    terrorists using, 98
    unmanned crafts as, 97

eagles
    drone attacked by, 98
    drones as nest for, 97
    French eagle squad with, *96*, 97, *97*
    Kevlar and leather protecting, 98

Earth
    atmosphere as marvel of, 55–56
    extraterrestrial not from, 89–90
    facts and stories on, 1
    fidget spinners and, 68, 70, 151
    gravity and sun orbited by, 68, 70
    green burial for health of, 74–76
    meteorite reaching, 86, *87*
    plate tectonics on, 12–13
    spin of, 69, *69*
earthquake
    disaster imagined like, 5
    explosion feeling like, 109
    Japan with large, 58, *58*
Eastern Siberia, Russia, 123
Edison, Thomas, 106
Einstein, Albert, 80, *80*
electrical signals
    brain with duplicated, 139
    EEG detecting brain, 130
    neurons transmitting, 140
    thoughts as, 137, 139
electricity
    air transmission of, 107, *107*
    hydroelectric dams producing, 30
    Tesla on, 106–7, *107*, 110
electroencephalogram (EEG), 130
energy
    kinetic motion as, *63*, *64*, 64–65,
        134–35
    nuclear power plant for, 59
    renewable, 133–34, 136, *136*, 157
engineers
    Google, 39
    machines and structures by, 63
entanglement

ACKNOWLEDGMENTS

How do you begin to write an acknowledgments page for a whole series of books? We think the safest, and truest, way to begin is simply this: Working on these books has been a dream come true. What started with the seed of an idea—"Look at these amazing creatures that exist/stories that have happened/places you would not believe!"—grew into a legacy of wonder and discovery that has topped our wildest imaginations.

We are so grateful for the incomparable team at Walden Press, who have outdone themselves at every step along the way and have truly been a joy to work with: Jordan Brown, Deborah Kovacs, Aurora Parlagreco, Bethany Reis, Megan Gendell, Alexandra Rakaczki, Caroline Sun, Alana Whitman, and so many more. Many thanks, also, to our agent, Erin Murphy, who has been with us through it all.

There is no end to the knowledge and generosity of the experts we have consulted as we have gone along in the writing and researching of these stories. To each and every one of you: our undying gratitude and respect, and we hope we have done your amazing stories justice. Any errors that may have snuck in are entirely our own.

To Danny Meldung and the entire team at Photo Affairs, who

secured all the necessary photo permissions—you are our heroes, and we couldn't have done it without you! Thanks also to Sammy Yuen, for creating the fake images for us, and to illustrator Lisa K. Weber, for giving the books both an adorable mascot and a creative sense of humor.

To our critique groups and beta readers, including Kevan Atteberry, Lois Brandt, Dori Hillestad Butler, Natalie Lorenzi, Curtis Manley, Jeanie Mebane, Julie Phillipps, Dan Richards, Allyson Valentine Schrier, Katie Slivensky, Dana J. Sullivan, Kip Wilson: Thanks for playing along and for all your thoughtful feedback along the way. We're also grateful to the Society of Children's Book Writers and Illustrators (SCBWI) for all they do to support children's books and their creators.

Much love and gratitude go to our families. Thank you for your unfailing support, which helps us keep doing what we so love to do.

To those individuals, institutions, and organizations that have shone your special spotlights on our series thus far: the Junior Library Guild, Chicago Public Library, ALA *Booklist*, Texas Topaz List, Maine Student Book Award committee, William Allen White Children's Book Award committee, Nerdy Book Club and Nerdies Award committee, and Cybils Award team—we thank you from the bottom of our hearts.

And last, but certainly not least, to every teacher, educator, librarian, parent, and reader who has loved and shared these books with others and who will continue to do so up ahead and on into the future: You are the reason we do what we do! We adore and thrive on each of your reviews, posts, and articles—and we especially love seeing all those action photos. Thank you for loving, reading, and sharing each of the books in the Two Truths and a Lie series!